RUN DADI RUN

RUN DADI RUN

DR GURJIT KAUR

Vitasta

Published by
Renu Kaul Verma
Vitasta Publishing Pvt Ltd
4348/4C, Ansari Road, Daryaganj
New Delhi - 110 002
info@vitastapublishing.com

ISBN: 978-81-19670-09-3
© Dr Gurjit Kaur
First Edition 2025
MRP ₹399

All Rights Reserved.
No part of this publication may be reproduced, stored in a retrieval system, or transmitted in any form, or by any means–electronic, mechanical, photocopying, recording or otherwise–without the prior permission of the publisher. Opinions expressed in this book are the author's own. The publisher is in no way responsible for these.

Edited by Reena Singh
Layout by Rohit Gautam
Cover Design by Somesh Kumar MISHRA
Printed at Chaman Enterprises, New Delhi

CONTENTS

Introduction		vii
Prologue: Unconditional Love		xv

Chapter 1:	Lonely Child	1
Chapter 2:	Family	7
Chapter 3:	Maharaja Bhupinder Singh	14
Chapter 4:	Divided India and Love	23
Chapter 5:	Gurdev with a Twist	36
Chapter 6:	God Proposes, Wo-Maan Runs!	43
Chapter 7:	One Step at a Time	49
Chapter 8:	Hollow Bones and a Fresh Start	52
Chapter 9:	A Novel Experiment	56
Chapter 10:	The First Run	61

Chapter 11:	Out of Patiala	67
Chapter 12:	Love and More Love at New Zealand	74
Chapter 13:	*Digdi Haan, te Jitdi Haan*—I fall, so I win!	84
Chapter 14:	Hole in a Pocket	92
Chapter 15:	What made Maan Run?	97
Chapter 16:	Maan's Secrets to Longevity	106
Chapter 17:	Maan, A Valued Celebrity!	126
Chapter 18:	Room Number One	134
Chapter 19:	Pinkathon	139
Chapter 20:	Immortal Messages for the Mortals	143
Chapter 21:	The Last Run	149

Epilogue: A Salute to a Special Woman	*159*
Annexure 1	*165*
Annexure 2	*167*
Acknowledgements	*169*
End Notes	*171*

INTRODUCTION

Ever since I was a child, my food preferences seemed to be completely different from the rest of my siblings. When they reached out for Maggi noodles, I would quietly fill my bowl with an extra helping of curd. When they piled their plates with mountains of rice, I preferred an extra helping of vegetables. I would start my day with almost a dozen pink guavas which, fortunately, for me grew year-round in our own backyard. This preference for healthy, sensible food was second nature to me, and sometimes I was the only one eating differently from my large, 20-member strong joint family.

I believe that it was this preference for healthy, natural foods that safeguarded me from the usual ailments that people all around me often succumbed to. I remember one incident when I was head girl during my hostel days. I was responsible for giving out medicines to my fellow hostelers, and perhaps it was those guavas that protected me from the virus which affected the whole wing, barring me. I remained standing strong and was able to protect the undergraduates who needed me. I believed that the foods that I ate also guaranteed equanimity in my behaviour. Moreover, my natural inclination towards fibrous fruits and vegetables somehow helped me to withstand the lure of packaged food.

Maybe it's my prior relationship with food that my soul remembers and has been carrying, perhaps since an eternity, but it prepared me for my future meeting with Maan Kaur. This was the reason why I was naturally attracted towards Maan and felt a strong connection with her.

OMG! Yeh Mera India, is a popular show on History TV18 that brings forth hidden wonders and implausible stories of several unsung characters from different parts of the country. An episode titled '101 and running' of this show was dedicated to Maan and her life.[1] That's when I learnt about Maan for the first time. I was fascinated by her achievements and seeing her running on the grounds of Punjabi University, Patiala literally gave me goosebumps! I was determined to meet her. Her simple yet inspiring lifestyle was enough to have my eyes well up with tears. Though I didn't share Maan's love for sports, I was in perfect sync with her passion to create awareness about the importance of a healthy lifestyle. That was the start of my own personal journey with Maan Kaur.

In March 2019, I got a chance to visit Punjabi University, Patiala, which was where Maan lived. Being a hotshot at the university campus, meant that locating her house was not a difficult task and soon I was at the door of her third-floor flat. With a single ring of the bell, Maan opened the door while her son, Gurdev, was cooking breakfast in the kitchen just opposite the flat's entrance.

We greeted each other. She had her hair hanging loose till her waist. 'I have washed my hair today,' Maan said by way of explanation.

She was wearing a white, loose knee-length shirt with a *salwar* (a pair of baggy, pleated trousers) and had covered her head with a scarf. Even her wet hair, left loose, had not stopped her from following the ancient tradition of covering one's head all the time. In north India, especially in rural areas, covering the head with a long *dupatta* mostly made of thin cotton or a light, gauzy material has been a tradition since hundreds of years. It is still mandatory to cover your head in religious places and in temples.[2]

Maan's charming smile enticed me and I was moved on seeing her at home in her simple flat in the university campus. Had I visited just a day earlier, I would have missed the chance of meeting her as she had returned from Poland just the night before.

A few days later, in April 2019, I found myself in Malaysia, where my husband had been transferred. I was still thinking about my meeting with Maan and during this time, I had watched many YouTube videos of *Biji* (as I would call her) performing in different countries—the more I saw, the more I came under the sway of this wonder-woman. I was now living in Malaysia and found myself with lots of free time. It was then that I discovered my true calling—and I decided to write about Maan and share her uplifting and motivating story with the world. My return to India this time had a motive—which was to meet Biji and thus, my second meeting, was filled with a sense of purpose.

My mind had been busy and I had already come up with a ground plan, but for that, I needed the support of both Maan and her son, Gurdev Singh. First, I broke the news to Gurdev that I was planning to write a biography on his mother's legendary life. Maan asked what the word 'biography' meant in the first place!

In the first meeting, she had assumed that I was an athlete who had come for training guidance, and during the second meeting, she thought I was a reporter who wanted to write a column about her in a newspaper. Then, Gurdev intervened, even as I was earnestly trying to explain the purpose of my meeting. He came up with a sample and holding the book in his hand, explained to his mom that I was there to know everything about her life and that I would be writing a book about her.

After that, I rapidly gained Maan's acceptance and Gurdev's broad smile indicated to her that he approved as well. That was what I was aiming to achieve, so I was happy too. I had been planning this for months, and my dream was finally coming true. In the meantime, I made notes of their upcoming commitments and fixed a date for our next meeting.

I lodged for a week as a paying guest at a place that was within walking distance of the university.

A phone call woke me up at 5 am, early the next morning. To my surprise, it was Biji who said, 'Would you like to accompany us to the grounds?' I got ready in record time and made my way to the university grounds.

This was the first time when I saw how Maan cherished every moment of her training sessions. Immediately after the training, she went grocery shopping with Gurdev and me, and I spent most of my waking hours with them throughout that week. Thus, from her early morning training sessions till night, I ended up eating all my three meals with Maan and her coach-son who defined the authenticity of my first-hand account of Maan—data that I recorded and also preserved in writing. Moreover, my Punjabi roots and understanding of her culture and language helped me to capture every emotion and understand Maan's way of thinking.

I observed and noted all that I could, even while Gurdev was flitting between the living room and the kitchen to share anything that popped up in his mind while preparing homecooked meals for us. Every morning spent with Maan was special and I felt privileged to receive her blessings which she continuously showered on me—like a queen distributing gifts in her kingdom without ever taking inventory of her stock. Apart from her blessings, in my first short meeting, itself, I was presented with a pair of pillow covers handcrafted by Biji. During my second visit after interviewing her, a toothbrush was offered to me, which she said she had gathered from her accommodation in a five-star deluxe hotel during one of her tournaments. She had neatly wrapped these complimentary items and carefully kept them under her mattress. That little symbolic gesture helped me to understand that for Maan, physical, mental, and even oral health was equally important.

I had to leave for Malaysia again and there I began writing the first few lines of my book on her. WhatsApp kept us in constant touch. Maan was always excited to share the news of all her achievements with me.

On 22 August 2019, I received a message at night that Maan had been invited to Delhi. Gurdev wrote:

'We have been invited by the PM office on 29 August where my mother would be honoured by the Prime Minister. We are reaching on 28 August and after the ceremony on 29 August, we will return to Chandigarh.'

Social media platforms—Facebook, Twitter, Instagram, YouTube among others, have made attempts to present Maan's life in a single video, post, or tweet but these limited videos would often fail to draw a connecting link between the world of social reality and the real-world in which Maan lived. Gurdev accompanied her during all her interviews, but bridging this gap was often a demanding task.

On the surface, the data available on the internet cannot always surmount the language barrier, and perhaps that is the reason why Maan's narration would sometimes get distorted, a fact corroborated by her son, Gurdev.

My last conversation with Biji was on 1 March 2021 on her 105th birthday which was celebrated with full fervour. Just after a few days, the unexpected news of her illness that took her life, broke the hearts of many.

Gurjit Kaur
November 2024

Maan Kaur with the author

PROLOGUE
UNCONDITIONAL LOVE

At the ripe old age of 105, Maan dreamt of her mother again and as she tried to touch her—to acknowledge her presence—she woke up with a start. Maan was used to travelling all over the globe and her mother would appear in her dreams and accompany her in her travels. Maan could calculate—in hours—the little time she had spent with her biological mother, but this fact never came in the way of their sublime mother-daughter relationship. A six-month-old Maan could hardly articulate what she had seen through her physical eyes, but the memories of her mother somehow stayed in her subconscious, ever fresh and vivid, far beyond those that could be captured by her five senses.

Maan neither wanted to understand nor ever tried to symbolically interpret the images she would see in her dreams. To put it in simple words, Maan would often dream of her mother simply because she missed her presence in her life. Were Maan's dreams flights of fancy through which she uncovered her raconteur skills or were they the crystallisation of the thoughts she had during the day? For many years, she confused the warmth of the thoughts of her mother with stories of spirits, but later, she trained her mind to view them without the illusion of fear clouding her thoughts.

In the course of time, once she had learnt to overcome her fear of what she had once perceived as the play of ghosts and goblins in her own mind, Maan's own personality and thoughts evolved. So, to feel her mother's presence, Maan would wait for nightfall, night after night. Daylight would take away the brightness of the only star in her life, but in the dark, it shone bright, guiding Maan through all her endeavours, till her last breath.

Living up to a healthful 105 years is a miracle in itself, but with Maan, the magic didn't end just here. The real miracle was Maan reaching the highest level of competitive games around the globe. Whether she was capable of performing miracles or not is another question, but the people who visited her undoubtedly believed that she could do that. There is this story narrated by a childless woman in her late thirties who was struggling to conceive despite the fibroids in her uterus. Tired of eating all sorts of prescribed medicines and almost at the verge of depression, the woman approached Maan. Today, she is mother to a three-year-old daughter. She said that she vested all her trust in Maan and that visit unlocked the doors to happiness for her entire family.[1]

Maan certainly received boundless grace from somewhere above. To earn these blessings, she didn't renounce the world or advocate the counting of rosaries to realise God. The only way that she adopted to find God was through practising 'Love.'

'Love Him not for the material things or for a comfortable life. Simply love and accept with respect, His entire creation,' Maan would often say.

Like a pledge, she believed this even on her worst rainy days. Her philosophy was simple, and she could endure all hardships, only because she ensured that there was no hole in her 'umbrella.' She loved her work and was in sync with her professional as well as household responsibilities. She respected not just the planet of which she considered herself to be but a small part, but also the various other planets and the entire Universe that she strongly believed in. Maan always wanted everyone to understand the essence of the One Universal Truth of Love as described by the tenth Sikh Guru, Sri Guru Gobind Singh:

Kaha Bhayo Jo Dou Lochan Mund Kai
Baith Rahio Bak Dhian Lagaaeo
Nhat Phirio Leeai Sat Samundran
Lok Gayo Parlok Gavaio
Bas Kio Bikhian So Baith Kai

> *Aise Hi Aise Su Bais Bitaio*
> *Sach Kahon Sun Leho Sabai*
> *Jin Prem Kio Tin Hee Prabh Paio*[2]
> **Sri Dasam Granth Sahib**

Translated, this verse means: 'Of what use it is, if one sits and meditates like a crane with his eyes closed. If he takes bath at holy places up to the seventh sea, he loses this world and also the next world. He spends his life in performing such actions and wastes his life in such pursuits. I speak Truth, all should turn their ears towards it: he, who is absorbed in True Love, he would realise the Lord.'

We live in a fast-paced world and have readily adopted western food habits. As a result, so many people are now suffering from hormonal imbalances, obesity, and several other health issues. Furthermore, the pandemic acted as a catalyst to spread additional stress with the onset of the novel, work-from-home trend. The world needs inspiration and hope to survive in these trying and changing times.

The legendary life of Maan Kaur can help uplift the spirits of readers and serve as a guide to attain higher spiritual realms. One of Maan's dreams was to assist the ageing population in seeking a meaningful life after retirement. The journey of the fastest and swiftest grandmother would also be a model to children, aspiring athletes, senior citizens, women and working mothers.

Thus, this book is not just a sports book providing insights about Maan's training regimen or a volume highlighting the awards the superwoman garnered. Youth and the present-day inhabitants of this world need guidance to maintain their physical and spiritual health, and Maan's life will help them achieve both these existential goals. Altering the lifestyle of just one person can bring a difference to an entire family. Hence, adopting the principles of Maan's life is quintessential to resolve the damages that the unconscious practices of the human race have caused to our cosmos. This book aims at serving the people of our country and the world at large.

Chapter 1

LONELY CHILD

1916 was labelled as a cursed year by the people of a small city, Patiala, in northern India. The Sidhu family who was living in this city around the same time were fighting their own demons and were beginning to acknowledge the rumours that a six-month-old baby girl born into their family was to be held responsible for her mother's death. Tarlok Singh believed that his newborn was a curse. She had devoured her mother Parsini Kaur; later, he married again, but three stepmothers of the little girl also passed away. This led to Tarlok Singh marrying five times!

The infamous Spanish influenza pandemic that hit India in 1918-19 has remained a neglected part of history inspite of the overwhelming fatalities it caused. One wonders if the deaths of Tarlok Singh's first three wives had anything to do with this pandemic. It must have been a time of devastation, coming as it did, just before the

First World War and other broader historical events. In this scenario, calculating the deaths in the Sidhu family would be a trivial task compared to the far gigantic socio-economic impact of this deadly disease which eventually claimed millions of lives even in India. But back then, it must have seemed easier to connect the deaths with Maan's birth because, as the family could argue for years, didn't her birth trigger the first death—that of Maan's mother?[1]

Maan Kaur, therefore, grew up with her working grandmother, who took care of her basic needs till she was small and couldn't fend for herself. Maan learnt, early on, that she shouldn't mess with her granny as she wasn't exactly a fount of love for the little girl. Her grandma worked in a school as an *aaya* (nanny) and was responsible for fetching around a hundred girls to school. However, she failed to persuade her own granddaughter to study.

Maan never developed any interest in going to school; she'd much rather play truant. On the few occasions when her grandma eventually triumphed in dragging her to school, she would run away before the teachers arrived. Subsequently, she learnt *Gurmukhi*—a script used by the Sikhs, when she was eight years old—and that too, at her father's initiative. She wasn't of much help to her grandma in managing household activities. In those days, even a child of five years was expected to cook, clean, and wash. If she failed to complete her domestic chores, the choicest of Punjabi abuses were thrown on to her, usually by her granny and occasionally by her father. Her stepmother added misery to her life by locking her in the house for the entire day without food. Being a cook who had been trained in British cuisine in the palace of Maharaja Bhupinder Singh, her father would not return home for weeks together, so, the young Maan was left at the mercy of these two women in her life. But a difficult childhood taught Maan several key survival strategies.

No one befriended Maan and villagers tagged her a *kalankini* (ill-reputed). People of the Hindu religion considered her presence an evil omen. They believed that talking to or accompanying her would bring bad omens to their house. With no one to play with, Maan would just roam around and passed her days playing games, all alone. The only traditional game that she played was *Geete Di Khed*, a game played with pebbles. She missed playing *Lukka Chhipee*, better known as hide and seek with other girls.

> **Maan—A Miracle Woman**
> Who knew back then that this little girl, whom the religious communities stridently snubbed, would one day turn out to be a Miracle Woman, who would literally inspire others with her own enthusiasm and be a role model for the world at large? No one predicted back then that one day, she would not just be a centenarian, but a celebrity runner giving tips to sundry others to improve physical fitness.

Dismissal from her own community led to her forming several inter-religious friendships—and she found solace in the company of a group of Muslim girls. Such alliances were common back then and were also found in the palace of the Maharaja of Patiala.[2] Glimpses into Maan's life are proof that communal trouble with the Muslims was illusory and was crafted by the British Raj, who modeled their governance on the Roman axiom of 'divide and rule.'[3] However, a polemic debate about clientage between Hindu-Muslim relations and the British rule is prevalent among social scholars.

Maan had seen the changing status of women from the beginning of the twentieth century till almost the first quarter of the twenty-first century. She was witness to times when women wore long dresses, when showing off their legs was considered to be taboo. She also saw the present age of bikinis, and she witnessed this at close hand during her worldwide tours as a sprinter. She had seen the days when women worked as cooks, clerks and waitresses in British India. She was three years old in 1919, the year when sex disqualification was dismissed.[4] Popularly known as the 'sacred year', 1919 was the year that opened doors for women to become solicitors, barristers, vets, and chartered accountants. In India, however, women, at that time, mostly relied on agriculture for their living and the female labour force further reduced due to the new protective legislation.[5] But a century, later, Maan together with the women of her nation had come a long way; 1916 to 2021, she had excelled as a centenarian in the World Masters Games. At the age of 105, she was an inspirational record holder in the 100 metres, 200 metres, shot put, and javelin throw. She proved to the world at large that age was just a number and in 2011, when she was ninety-five, she received the 'Athlete of the year,' title.

Though born in a period of great triumph and tragedy, Maan eventually learnt the art of shining even in mayhem. She represented the philosophy of 'simple living and high thinking' in its truest form—without a lengthy laundry list of 'do's and don'ts.' A visitor would never go empty-handed from her house, even those who were just paying her a flying visit. She frequently crafted her own gifts and gave these to her guests, even if all she had to give away at a certain time was a neatly packed toothbrush kept under her mattress.

Despite such a rocky childhood, she grew up gracefully and became an epitome of elegance, charm and a great motivator for the youth of today. While sharing her life story, Maan kept an equanimous face throughout, and seemed to have distanced herself from the unrestrained criticism that she often faced from her own family members.

Tips from Maan's Life to Combat Loneliness:
1. Accept your situation even if you feel socially ignored
2. Distance yourself from fault-finding people. Even Saint Kabir Das left Banaras and moved to Maghar during his last days[6]
3. Explore and connect with nature
4. Choose an outdoor game that you can play alone
5. Be open to form close associations with people outside your community

Chapter 2

FAMILY

Illiteracy proved a boon for Maan. It ensured her a simple mindset free from complex thoughts or a tendency towards critical analysis. She had no inclination for numbers, either. Because of this, life was simple with few knots to unravel. Her childhood and adulthood were demarcated with just one life-changing incident—marriage. Before the age of eighteen years, her age at the time of her marriage, she thought of herself as a child and the very next day of marriage, she became an adult.

Marriage was a conservative affair and the elders did not ask for her consent when they were choosing her groom. That was against the cultural norms set by the society of those times. For this reason, she had had only a brief look at her groom when he uncovered her *ghunghat* (a veil covering the face). All she knew was the crisp wedding dress she would slip into and that she was marrying a man by the name of Ranjit Singh who hailed from the same city, Patiala. Calling her husband by his name was not permitted in those days.

She wore a long-pleated skirt with a blouse popularly known as *ghagra choli*. It was made up of one complete *thaan* (a piece of cloth ten metres long) on her wedding day. The wedding ceremony was grand, with celebrations spread over four days. Food was traditional and was prepared at home. There were seven types of sweets besides a variety of dishes all made by her father in their open kitchen. Serving *khichdi* (a dish made with rice and lentils) to the bridegroom's family as a welcoming dish was believed to bring good fortune and a promising future. Accordingly, this dish was served to the guests at the time of the marriage.

Her husband was a peon who later on, took on the post of a qualified Indian cook at the palace of Maharaja Bhupinder Singh. Professionally, he was a specialised cook, but he never assisted Maan in her kitchen, as only the lady of the house was responsible for preparing meals for the family. It was a general norm to speak less and not indulge in any kind of long conversations with one's husband, back in those days.

Fortunately, pregnancy required no exchange of words! As a result, she delivered four children in her lifetime. The first was a daughter who passed away shortly after her birth. The second, was a boy, Gurdev Singh followed by another boy, Manjit Singh. The fourth child was a daughter, Amrit Kaur who now lives in Chandigarh.

The children kept her busy with household tasks. Her daily chores would begin at 4 am in the morning. Serving tea to the entire family including her in-laws was her first task for the day and it took priority even over her children. She was not only an excellent homemaker, but also knew the importance of earning money as she always fancied that she was skilled with her hands. This filled her with a certain sense of confidence, giving a boost to her personality.

She was a woman with limited needs who, otherwise led an austere life and this even reflected in the choice of clothes and fabric that she wore daily. She wore *khaddar* (handloom plain-weave cotton fabric) clothes, which had also been worn by Saint Kabir Das, a fifteenth century mystic poet. Summers or winters, *khaddar* was the preferred cloth which was later introduced by Mahatma Gandhi as the symbol of the nationalist movement as the masses could easily identify with it.[1] Thus khaddar, was not just a fabric, but was referred to as the 'fabric of Indian Independence.'[2] Khadi was a symbol of simplicity introduced with an aim to promote Indian value systems, and Gandhi clearly expressed his emotions in the following extract published in *Young India* in 1925:

'The message of the spinning-wheel is much wider than its circumference. Its message is one of simplicity, service of mankind, living so as not to hurt others, creating an indissoluble bond between the rich and the poor, capital and labour, the prince and the peasant.'[3]

Maan was eight when she first sensed the importance of money. By choice, she had resolutely stayed away from school, but varied lucrative opportunities had opened their doors to her. Back in those days, there were no professional courses or vocational, job-oriented courses available for women. It was the first few years of the Great Depression and the economic and political impact of it was seen on India in the 1930s, which further influenced subsequent events in the country.[4] In this turmoil, the only way to learn was through on-the-job training. Maan, who believed that she was born to toil, tried her hand at almost a dozen crafts. Weaving drawstrings for *salwars* was her first job and she received a paisa for each drawstring. Her tiny hands interlaced the warp and weft with swift strokes to earn a living from weaving. Spinning the thread for handloom weavers in the mud house where she lived, became a regular job. She was good with her hands and had even helped her father to build a mud house, too!

Milling wheat and fashioning natural toothbrushes from the twigs of the Neem tree, commonly known as *datuns* were some of the other jobs that Maan tried. She kept on earning those coins and deposited them in her *bugni,* the Punjabi word to describe a piggy bank. Not knowing how big her bank account had become in the past ten years, she carried her piggy bank to her nuptial house.

On being asked how much money she had collected, she would reply, '*Pata nai kinne paise kathe kitte par bugni bahut bharhi ho gayi, si*'—I don't know how much I earned, but my piggy bank was heavy when I turned eighteen.'

Following her husband's and father's footsteps, she, too, started working as a cook after marriage. She was fond of preparing north-Indian cuisine for wedding ceremonies. As she recounted her stories about her time as a cook, I could see her eyes light up! She described vividly how the complete pot of *khichdi* and curd made for a hundred people would be over in a trice. *Panjeeri,* a sweet prepared with whole wheat flour and popular in north India during winters, was her favourite sweet filled as it was with crunchy dry fruits, seeds, a dash of Vedic herbs and edible gum.

Maan had skills to create almost everything a man needed for survival: *roti* by milling wheat, *kapda* by weaving cloth and even building a *makaan* or house. Giving shape to the fabric that she could so easily weave was next on her list of skills that she mastered and in no time, she was able to stitch a *salwar-kameez* and other dresses. Maan, was exceptionally brilliant with her hands and required no fashion designer course to learn this art. Fetching a pot of water from the well to the house of the tailor was her learning stratagem and acted as her barter system! In exchange for delivering water, she learnt a new skill from the tailor and soon, she was crafting and styling her own clothes. She then experimented with many more household and domestic items, including making and designing quilts, mattresses and creating decorative borders for bedsheets.

Until the age of 105, Maan continued her craft and with great delight designed pillow covers. She was able to thread her own needles with help from her thick myopic glasses, and would even manage to insert thread into the eyelet of the thin needle of her sewing machine. These pillow covers were priced at Rs 150 each and she was strict on her principles and would allow no bargaining. Her commonsense approach was apparent in the many valuables that she had crafted with a fusion of leftover fabrics. Till her last breath, this wonder woman was spotted in her handmade salwar-kameez which she would wear with aplomb even at grand global interview platforms. She was fairly detached from her celebrity testimonials and pursuits.

> **Stop Whining, Shrug Away Your Problems!**
> Maan never questioned her life and the various twists and turns it took over a century. Raised without the support of her parents, she welcomed everything that came in her life as a *Hukam* (divine order). She lived in harmony with the laws of nature and this foundation made her life simple and at the same time, gave her strength to bear the world's atrocities. This trait in her

character helped her to swallow her grandma's Punjabi curses as well as bear the many times her father would hit her for being a proverbial slugabed. She didn't even whine about all these embarrassing moments! Moreover, she dismissed these experiences smilingly with a shrug and described the men in her life with a philosophical: *'Ou gaalan da zamana si dono bande danda maran vale miley.'* Explicitly translated, it means that using abusive language and beatings was a trend in those days and both her father and husband displayed these traits.

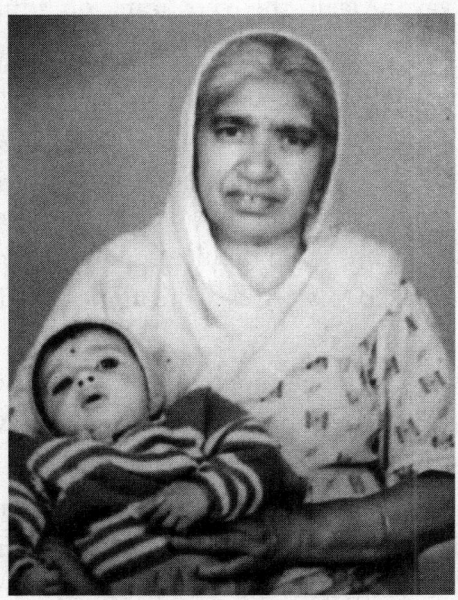

Maan Kaur with her grandson

Chapter 3

MAHARAJA BHUPINDER SINGH

Marriage gave Maan the certificate of adulthood. It qualified her to work as a nanny and a professional caretaker in the Maharaja's palace. Maharaja Bhupinder Singh of the princely state of Patiala, belonged to the Phulkian dynasty.[1] Like most of the Indian nawabs and rulers, his reign was famously titled as *Sarkar-e-Inglishia*. He led a lavish life in an architecturally designed palace where he stocked his wives, concubines, maidservants, mistresses and caretakers.[2]

Maharaja Narinder Singh, the great-grandfather of Bhupinder Singh had built the magnificent Moti Bagh Palace which was often compared with buildings in Versailles. In this palace, Bhupinder Singh was believed to maintain a harem of 332 women of whom ten were recognised as the Maharanis and about fifty more as his Ranis. The rest were either mistresses or servants.[3] His progeny from his many wives and many concubines, were more than eighty.[4] However, Diwan J Dass in his book, *Maharaja*, claims the presence of at least three hundred women in the palace. Doctors visited the palaces of the Maharanis, the Ranis and the other women for routine health checks. Identifying each one of them by their names was a cumbersome task so the women were enumerated in alphabetical order, with even the Maharanis represented as A, B, C, D, E, F and so on. A numeral system was used to tell the Ranis apart, so they were known as 1, 2, 3, 4, 5, 6, 7, 8, 9…till the file number had reached 150. Even more women were mentioned in the chart as A1, A2, B1, B2, C1, C2 etc.[5] Commoners were not permitted to witness these pleasures of the Maharaja, and everyone around him, including Maan very well knew about his consorts and extravagance, something that is well-documented and known to the world.

Yet, Maan did not confirm or deny about the numbers allotted to the women in the palace. All she said was: *'Kuriya ginti te nai aundiya si'*, it was hard to keep a count of the number of women around the maharaja. But she did describe the sumptuous parties which were thrown for viceroys, governors, residents and English aristocrats where tiger and duck shoots, pig-sticking, polo matches and nautch performers for the guests were arranged.[6]

Maan had closely witnessed the Patiala Maharaja's extravagant lifestyle, and she passionately recalled those memories and reminisced about the old days when they waited for hours sometimes, for a fleeting look at the Maharaja in his motorcade of twenty Rolls-Royces.[7] Maharaja Bhupinder Singh is well-known for building 'Patiala State Monorail Trainways,' and also owned the first aircraft in India and had an airstrip built at Patiala.[8]

As a part of the palace staff, Maan had the unique opportunity to closely witness the lives of the queens. She had distinct memories of them and described their exquisite jewellery to me, almost ninety years later, in vivid detail. Remembering the colourful chiffon Patiala salwars and *sarees* that the queens favoured would bring a smile to her face. The scenes that Maan described were unlike the other princely states like Rajasthan, where women lived in *purdah,* wearing a veil to hide their faces from the public. But here in Patiala, the women enjoyed a more colourful and lavish lifestyle.

Maan's countenance took on a coy look as she described the men in the palace as tall, dark, and handsome with their pale pink Patiala turbans and *achkans*—this formal designer knee-length jacket was a regular dress worn by men in those days.

She even remembered the famous 'Patiala Necklace' which the Maharaja commissioned to the House of Cartier for designing because of their expertise in intricate French savoir-faire.[9] He was a lavish, playboy maharaja fond of both jewellery and western designs. Maan shared her excitement and memory of the time he had gifted a splendid ruby and pearl necklace specially designed by Cartier to Rani Yoshoda Devi. The portrait of the Rani sporting the necklace at the Vandyk Studios in London is proof of the Maharaja's liking for exquisite jewellery.[10] She even recalled the eventful day when a studio was set up for the Maharaja and his queens to get clicked at the Patiala Palace!

With pride in her voice, Maan said '*Darkhotiwale Raniya di sewa kitti hai*'—I have served the queens of Darkoti.

All the queens belonging to a particular region were allotted a specific area and they lived together in the *Zenana* (harem). The queens whom Maan had served lived in the main Moti Bagh Palace together with the Maharaja, while his harem queens lived in the Lalbagh Palace in the palace grounds. The front face of the palace was adorned by Rajasthan-style *jharokas* and *chhatris* and while back then, it was a rare sight, now visitors can see it without restrictions as the erstwhile Moti Bagh palace now houses the National Institute for Sports, Patiala.

She was fond of her queens; she said it was like a dream for a girl in her early twenties to serve them. She looked forward to going to work daily, devotedly serving these young, elegant, and beautiful queens and their royal children. Specifically, she was one of the twelve caretakers working for a single queen. The caretakers lived together in the Moti Bagh Palace in a separate wing. She was assigned to dedicatedly look after the safety of the children apart from bathing and feeding them their meals and cleaning their rooms. Dealing with the tantrums of these royal children was part of her job. Nursing the queen and providing timely medicines to her was also part of her responsibilities. Maan silently took in these unique experiences. In turn, these helped her in learning about herself and life! It was not only about a set of duties that she had to execute, but she also equally enjoyed her role of a nanny.

Moreover, she was happy to be with the other royal caretakers. Many friendships were forged between them. She learnt to receive and give affection to her peers.

The children met their mothers in the *Zenana*, a part of the palace reserved for women, a few times a week. On other days, the little ones were dependent on Maan's care and warmth. Her infectious smile was like a ray of the bright sun in a nurtured garden for these children and they reciprocated her warmth and affection. The children would meet their father from time to time—meetings that mainly brought them material benefits. The Maharaja would take them to a huge room full of toys and the children could pick any number of goodies that they wanted. Maan savoured these moments when she accompanied these children. She herself had received neither love nor toys from her own father.

Maan was known for her valour and daring attitude

amidst the palace workers. An incident she recalled fondly was that of climbing a high mountain during the night, leaving her mates behind. She wasn't scared of beasts or wild animals as her own life experiences had trained her to be bold and to be at home with the unexpected. She aimed to reach the tallest mountain and greeted every new day as the beginning of a new adventure in which she would scale yet another new peak.

Among the queens of the Darkoti region, Maan was among the most sought-after nanny. Each one wanted Maan to accompany them on their evening walk. She would engage them with her stories culled from her ordinary life and proved to be a great entertainer. This gave her a subtle advantage over the other caretakers. During her lonely childhood days, she had developed these raconteur skills. She lived in her own, imaginary world that was nevertheless very real to her. The words and feelings she could not share with others in her growing years stayed in her budding mind, and now came alive as she regaled the queens with her stories.

This role as a nanny in which she was sought after by the royal household helped her outgrow her feelings of being unwanted and disliked by people in her earlier life before she was married. The painful, unrequited memories of love of her family were now more than compensated and reciprocated by her colleagues in the Maharaja's palace. Her work was appreciated and this helped build her confidence. Trust was the foundation of her relationship with the queens and she vowed to preserve it. The queens, without any hesitation would allow Maan to try on their jewellery or dance with their chiffon *dupattas*—a long piece of rectangular cloth meant to be used as a long scarf to cover their head and shoulders. As everyone knows, the dupatta is an integral part of an Indian woman's attire and symbolically protects her modesty. A woman who wears this commands respect and prompts people to keep their distance!

***

Chail and Kandaghat

The entire palace would set off for Chail and Kandaghat as the Maharaja shifted his residence during summers. Maan would also accompany the queens along with the consorts, maid servants, mistresses, caretakers and over four hundred dogs on their summer visits to the Chail Palace which later received heritage status by the Ministry of Tourism.[11] Maharaja Bhupinder Singh was famous for his love for bold architecture; his palaces and surrounding buildings were constructed keeping his preference for this architectural style in mind. Especially striking were the Kali Temple in Patiala, the Chail View Palace, Oakover and the Cedar Lodge in Shimla. It was thanks to the maverick Maharaja that the Chail Palace began to serve as the summer retreat of the rich and the mighty. Given his love for cricket, the Maharaja had the world's highest cricket pitch built here, at a height of 2,144 metres in 1893.[12] Patiala XI and Patiala Tigers, the polo and cricket teams sponsored by the Maharaja marked their presence worldwide, asserting his love for sports.[13]

Strains of melodious, vintage music often played in the palace, exhibiting a royal way of life that she had never imagined in her childhood. This new life left a very positive impact on Maan's life. Later, she even began looking forward to her queen's pleasure and recreational activities especially ballroom dancing where music would blare from vinyl records, something she described simply as, *'Tawa, wajda hunda si.'* She would liken records to the Indian *tawa*, a black iron round-shaped disc used in the kitchen to dry-roast Indian bread.

More magnificent happenings were the lavish weddings celebrated in the palace. For Maan, it was like watching a complete theatrical production with accompanying pomp and glory. The choicest of Indian cuisine and sweets were prepared and a musical band and dance were the central theme of these celebrations. Maan, together with the staff would mimic these classical episodes in the absence of the Maharaja when he would be away on his foreign visits.

The year 1938, however, brought an abrupt end to Maan's life in the opulent palace of the Maharaja. The king passed away in March 1938 at the age of forty-seven![14] The employees working at the palace and Maan's family were, fortunately, saved from unemployment. Her husband got the privilege to serve in a government office in Punjab. Later, the family moved to Chandigarh, which led to the beginning of a new chapter in Maan's life.

Chapter 4

DIVIDED INDIA AND LOVE

Indians expected self-governance in exchange for their contributions in the Second World War. However, inter-communal violence among the Hindus, Muslims, and Sikhs erupted as an unforeseen consequence of freedom. To secure the acquiescence of both the Muslim League and the Indian National Congress, partition was the only option. Maan's sensitive nerves raised just one question; was partition really necessary? Did it happen because of the rising communal tensions in the 1930s, because of the political decisions made by the leaders at both the national and provincial levels, in the aftermath of the Second World War, and as an impact of the 'Great Calcutta Killing,' which led to the breakdown of law and order in 1946? Or was it just something that was bound to happen, given the involvement of both the Muslim League and the Indian National Congress?[1] Despite the reasons, Maan never believed that India should have been so sliced. But Lord Mountbatten, Jinnah, and Nehru had other plans and were sharpening their axes to slice their motherland.[2] Maan, personally, had a strong opinion about this and would often insist that India was, till then, united and could never be sliced into two!

Maan saw the turmoil and bloodshed that resulted during the Partition and remembered the chaotic movement of millions who moved to the other side of the borders. Maan was thirty-one at the time when India gained independence. Millions of people became refugees and the loud cries of torture, gunshots, lathis, and the heartbreaking stories of how her friends and neighbours were slaughtered disturbed Maan, and her recollections of those times, even after seventy-four years of Independence, would shake her equilibrium.

In the decade before the Partition, when Maan was still in her twenties, she would often try to make sense of the non-cooperation and peasant movements, and of events that had taken place in the early 1920s, when she was only a little girl. Peasant discontent had majorly broken out in her birthplace, Patiala and she would listen to stories that her father told her about the Left leaders, Bhagwan Singh Longowalia, Jagir Singh Joga, and Teja Singh Sutantar who wanted restoration of land illegally seized through trickery and threats. These leaders were actively involved in the Muzara movement demanding land ownership rights from the zamindars, the British authorities, and the kings.³ The Left leaders had incited the muzaras or tenants to refuse to pay the *batai* or rent to their *biswedars,* landlords.

On 11 March 1947, compelled by the Muzara movement, the Maharaja of Patiala had announced a royal proclamation which guaranteed proprietorship rights to the tenants only on a portion of the land. The tenants refused to accept this and insisted on the return of their hereditary land.⁴ The struggle continued until 1953—when finally, legislation in favour of the tenants was passed.⁵ She believed that the stories that her father shared with her helped strengthen her emotionally.

But her simple mind still failed to understand the need for Partition and the greed for power that gave birth to the two new nations—only to embark on a new war over the princely state of Kashmir. Accounts of ghost trains that carried corpses of Hindus and Sikhs who hurriedly fled to India, and of Muslims travelling towards Pakistan horrified Maan and she kept abreast of whatever was happening around her.

Fortunately, Maan could read Gurmukhi, the Punjabi script, and was able to read the accounts of what was happening around her. The newly established newspapers, *The Tribune, Akal Parkash, Punjabi Darpan, Sudharak, Chitar Pattar,* and *Shaheed* expressed resistance to British colonial rule, and were used as weapons against them.⁶

With the advent of eighty newspapers in the province, the first half of the twentieth century was a vibrant period in the history of the northwest region of Indian journalism. However, the majority of newspapers did not last for more than a year.[7] She began reading newspapers aloud, sitting on the concrete that enclosed the base of the Banyan or the sacred *Peepal* trees near her house. Those who could not afford two *annas* (Indian currency worth one-sixteenth of a rupee) to buy a newspaper or were illiterate, surrounded Maan. This motivated many to learn Gurmukhi so that they could read the news at their own pace. Consequently, Punjabi newspapers gained popularity and were sold in black.[8] She was particularly fond of the *Patiala Samachar*, a fortnightly which was first published in Patiala state in 1944.[9] The household would always have a copy of this newspaper.

Punjab was divided into East and West Punjab as an outcome of the Partition. This fractured the strong economic, socio-political, and religious roots of the once solid and strong United Punjab before the division.[10] The partition and the Boundary Commission Award declared on 12 August 1947, had disheartened the Sikh community as the demarcation had failed to consider their religious, historical and emotional factors, in which several of their sacred shrines became a part of West Punjab that was in Pakistan. The Radcliffe Award also stirred up controversy among historians, civil servants and public men in Pakistan. West Punjab accused the Viceroy, Lord Mountbatten of being in collusion with Sir Cyril Radcliffe, Chairman of the Boundary Commission and altering the Punjab boundary at the last stage. Pakistan was dissatisfied as thirteen districts that included Ambala, Jalandhar, Amritsar, Pathankot, Gurdaspur, and Batala were allotted to East Punjab. Mountbatten was further criticised for his alleged involvement in pressuring Radcliffe, in allotting the Muslim-majority areas of Gurdaspur and Batala in Gurdaspur district and Ferozepur, Zira, and Fazilka in Ferozepur district to India which majorly uprooted the Muslims present in these parts and also in the adjoining towns of Qadian in Batala. This is attributed, in part, to Jinnah's refusal to appoint Mountbatten as the Governor-General of Pakistan after the partition of India.[11]

Maan was fortunately on the native side of the border, but her Muslim friends unfortunately now found that they had to leave and travel to the opposite side. Her only companions during her lonely childhood had now become victims of this massacre. During the British Raj, Maan had happily served the English community as her young, inexperienced mind was too naïve and innocent to understand the implications of the Crown rule over India. But even she could not bear how the entire nation had to pay the price for winning their freedom from the British Crown.

The dissolution of the Raj was marked as the most

momentous and emotional event in the history of the subcontinent. The newly independent states witnessed mass migration across the borders and around twenty million people were displaced.[12] Maan was separated from her friends falling under the province of Pakistan and as a consequence, people belonging to Rawalpindi, Lahore, Karachi, and Peshawar had to leave India. In a matter of months, the landscape of South Asia had changed irrevocably. The division uprooted 47.6 per cent of Hindus in Karachi and one-third of Muslims in Delhi—two hundred thousand Muslims left the Capital of India.[13]

The abandoned Hindu and Sikh properties opened up new avenues for profiteering and corruption in Pakistan and local residents were quick to illegally occupy 36 per cent of the shops and more than 50 per cent of the abandoned houses that Indians had left behind in Pakistan.[14]

Maan's entire family and neighbours who consisted of Hindus, Sikhs, Christians, and Buddhists helped their many Muslim friends to cross the borders.

One day, her husband, Ranjit Singh brought the depressing news that Maan's childhood friend and the lone witness of her nocturnal mountain treks—had been molested brutally. Ranjit Singh had witnessed the whole incident at the railway station where Maan's friend, Chanduni was tortured and killed, and he was sincerely apologetic for not being able to help her. While seeing hordes of Hindus approaching his daughters, Chanduni's husband chose to kill them with his own hands to prevent their sexual assault, abduction or being sold into prostitution. The whole family was, therefore, found slain in an instant.

Women, everywhere are held in high esteem and are a symbol of respect and purity, but they are also weak and cannot defend themselves against a rampaging mob who thinks that besmirching a woman's honour is the easiest way to show their superiority.

The horrifying details of how Chanduni and her family were killed left a lifetime scar on Maan's soul. It took months for her to recover, but eventually, life moves on and so did Maan. She didn't receive any news about her other companions, and thus believed that the rest were safe and had reached their destination. She wanted to live with this belief. The vindictive attitude of the people from both sides of the border, all in the name of religion— Hindus Vs. Muslims distressed Maan, but the spine-chilling stories of people and families being brutally killed kept coming. The very next day, her father reported the carnage of several Muslim cooks who had been working in the palace with him in their bid to flee to Pakistan.

The rich were fortunate as they could afford to get away in their private transport with guards, but the local labourers, domestic workers and poor inhabitants who had to rely on train services were callously murdered. She took time to recover from the shock of what had happened as the Partition left Maan's beloved Punjab bleeding, and she carried the burden of this separation in her heart, forever.

Many from Lahore escaped to Shimla with the hope of returning to their motherland, after the riots. But the partition line declared Lahore as a part of Pakistan and none of the families could return. They ended up permanently migrating to the tranquil hill stations of India, mainly Shimla, Mussoorie, and Dehradun.[15] Though Shimla was the city where the foundation of the Partition was laid down, people still trusted this city more than other parts of the country. The round table at the Viceregal Lodge is a testimony to the historical events that divided the country. Many of the Punjab Government's offices that were situated in Lahore were moved to Shimla.[16] The government of Himachal Pradesh took over the Chail Gurudwara Sahib which was built by Maharaja Bhupinder Singh and for use as a holy place by the Sikh community.[17] Maan had fond memories of her prayers being answered at this gurudwara before the nation gained its Independence.

> **Pockets of Hope**
> Maan described the whole process of the division of the country as meaningless and traumatic that uprooted people from their birthplaces and their communities. It separated Maan from her childhood friends with whom she had shared countless little adventures. Long after the Partition, she nurtured the hope that one day she

> would cross the border in search of her loved ones. Later, she realised that the border line was impassable, that one now needed a passport and a visa to see her friends and that the relationship between the newly formed countries which once upon a time, shared a soul had now only bitterness and hatred for each other.

'We, Hindus and Muslims, coexisted without conflict until the political leaders tainted our innocent minds. Though all religions preach humanity and believe in One Creator, our minds were negatively conditioned by focusing only on the differences between us. The diversity which we once enjoyed, soon turned into hatred and very soon, they divided us on religious, social, and traditional grounds,' added Maan. She described it as one of the greatest migrations human history had ever seen.

***

First Loves—Bhagat Singh and Saint Randhir Singh

Bhagat Singh, one of the youngest social revolutionaries India had ever seen and a staunch freedom fighter not only left a profound impact on the Indian freedom movement but also influenced Maan deeply. The Jallianwala Bagh massacre site, in particular, was the catalyst that profoundly touched Bhagat Singh. He visited the site with his family, who revered Mahatma Gandhi.[18] He was further influenced by the non-cooperation movement and the Ghadar resistance. These two movements left such an indelible impact on his mind that he decided to leave school to devote his life to the cause of fighting for the independence of India.[19] Reading about his brave stories, Maan learnt to be fearless and to face the consequences of the choices one makes in life. Once, during the course of my long chats with Maan, she remembering her childhood role model, uttered enthusiastically, *'Inquilab Zindabad'*. Inquilab Zindabad—long live revolution was a slogan for freedom and justice—that resounded through the streets.[20] Maan was in love with *Shaheed-e-Azam* Bhagat Singh's daring mindset. She constantly read about him in newspapers and kept herself informed about him, besides maintaining her own scrapbook about his records and personal reports of all the events in his struggle for India's freedom.

Bhagat Singh's passion for life and truth was observed in the various college plays that he performed; however, it was his obsession to see India gain freedom that made him a hero in real life. She was fascinated by his life, even though she knew that guns were his favourite companions. But he had an equally great flair for poetry and was an avid reader. He voraciously read about European revolutionaries and tried to fashion his own revolutionary actions on their examples. The throwing of two bombs in the Central Assembly and the Lahore Conspiracy Case brought him into the national limelight. Her hero was soon arrested for these very same offences and ironically, he became even more popular after his death sentence. He was hanged in the Lahore Central Jail. This incident left an irreplaceable void in Maan's life and she always regretted that she could never meet her first love, Bhagat Singh. His extraordinary life taught Maan to live life like a lioness, but she attributed her spiritual success to another political leader, Saint Randhir Singh.

Randhir Singh was also a political freedom fighter and a 'Ghadarite' who vigorously participated in the armed revolution against the British Government for India's Independence. He was a learned scholar with expertise in Punjabi, Brij (a dialect of the Braj region), Urdu, Persian, and English. His Urdu and Punjabi poetry completely altered Maan's approach towards spirituality, and broadened her religious beliefs.

Randhir Singh endured several unprecedented hardships and illnesses with stoicism. He maintained his poise through meditation and *samadhi* (intense self-absorption) in the various jails of India during his life imprisonment for the Lahore Conspiracy Case from 1915-30.[21] All the physical pain and torture exercised by the jail authorities failed to touch his spiritual soul.

Both these compassionate men who deeply impacted Maan were scholars, who were spiritually and socially active. They attained self-mastery and sacrificed their lives for the whole of humanity. With their sensitive souls, they wrote poetry—one in love for his country, and the other in praise of the divine. Both were passionate lovers, and it was hard to curb their free-spirited souls by imprisoning them behind bars. Maan lived under the influence of her two role models, and with time, her overall personality kept on transforming. Yet, Maan could never reconcile the major dissimilarity in her heroes.

'Meeting with Bhagat Singh, The Great Patriot,' a chapter in the *Autobiography of Bhai Sahib Randhir Singh*, and 'Why I am an Atheist,' an essay written by Bhagat Singh in the Lahore Central Jail revealed two completely diverse aspects of the young Maan's most important role models of her young days in their views of the Omniscient Lord. But what disturbed Maan the most was the uncertainty of her two protagonists.

Both men were lodged in the same jail, and on Bhagat Singh's appeal, who was waiting for his execution, he asked to meet Randhir Singh prior to his release from Lahore prison. Bhagat Singh confessed to Randhir Singh that he was an atheist. After a long conversation, Bhagat Singh's outlook towards spirituality completely changed, claimed Randhir Singh who wrote in his autobiography:

'So now you will be extremely pleased to learn that your dear Bhagat Singh is a believer in God, and he will die with complete spiritual faith in Sikhism, and according to the Sikh terminology, I will face not death but ascension.'[22]

Bhagat Singh in his essay, 'Why I Am an Atheist,' however, replied:

'One of my friends asked me to pray. When informed of my atheism, he said, 'During your last days, you will begin to believe.'

I said, 'No, dear sir, never shall it happen. I consider it to be an act of degradation and demoralisation. For such petty selfish motives, I shall never pray.'[23]

Maan stressed on the dialogue between the two outstanding intellectual personalities that took place behind the bars of the Lahore Central Jail. She couldn't understand this discourse between her two heroes and preferred to leave it to the intellectuals to explain such issues. She wanted to rever and love her two idols with fervour and passion.

Chapter 5

GURDEV WITH A TWIST

Chandigarh was newly designed by the Swiss French architect, Le Corbusier when Maan with her family relocated to the city. In her earlier life in Patiala, she had shouldered all sorts of responsibilities, whether it was taking care of household chores, looking after the children, or working at the Maharaja's palace. She adored her work and realised its importance in balancing her physical and psychological needs. She felt that work added to her confidence and contributed to her social identity. She was endowed with a plethora of talents and could not wait to begin work, so finding employment in this modern new city became her mission. All she needed was some thread and a sewing machine and she would be in business!

Her free-spirited nature and her interest in learning anything new had so far come to her rescue, but in the city, Maan realised the importance of formal education in acquiring a respectable white-collar job.

'For growth in one's career, a professional degree is inevitable which further helps in providing stability in life,' she would hear Ranjit Singh tell his sons.

Had Maan not forced her children to go to school, or if Ranjit Singh had behaved indifferently, their children would not have grown up as capable and competent adults. So, she thought it best that her children get a well-rounded, systematic and traditional system of education. She believed that this would help instil values and the sophisticated skills they needed in the modern world for survival. The move to Chandigarh opened brilliant possibilities for Maan's children to upgrade their potential. They now had the opportunity to access formal education and enjoy the amenities that a modern city offers for learning, growth, and development.

Shortly after Maan arranged for her sewing machine, she was soon fashioning five-metre long cloth into a fashionable salwar-kameez. Maan would sew while her children were at school. Most of Maan's contemporaries chose to wear sarees (five-and-a-half-metres of drape) worn always with a petticoat and blouse. Back in those days, women wore *ghagras* and sarees, before the arrival of the Punjabi suit.[1] The salwar of this Punjabi suit had its genesis in Patiala, and the Patiala salwar is worn even today. Maan had already learnt to stitch this traditional dress during her childhood in Patiala, but she needed to publicise her skills among the people of Chandigarh. She was lucky and several women in her neighbourhood showed interest in her art. Maan became a walking advertisement for the flowing, loose, voluminous Patiala salwars that she gracefully wore as her friends and neighbours started noticing her. And so, she began crafting reams of cloth into elegant shapes and would even stitch for her friends when they could not afford to pay her.

She narrated the first time this happened, when a friend told her: *'Kapda mera, naap mera, te paise kaade lene? Sirf dhaga te hi ae!'* Translated, this would mean, 'The cloth is mine, the body measurements are mine, and so what do you need money for? It's just a thread that you've invested in!'

Gurdev, her second-born would watch his mother toiling for the next sixty years in Chandigarh, but he never tried to stop her from stitching. He knew his mother was a workaholic and that she could not rest between household chores. Now that she was ninety-three, her strength and stamina was not less than that of the young woman who had shifted to Chandigarh in her thirties. Furthermore, her mental faculties were also as sharp as ever.

Seventy-one-year-old sprinter Gurdev was well aware of his mother's enthusiastic nature. His own love for athletics began in school and continued till he graduated. Gurdev had participated in various events until he started his own professional career at the Punjab Agricultural University (PAU), Ludhiana. During this phase, his love for sports took a back seat, but his deep love for field and track events once again sprouted in the early 2000s. He decided to take a temporary break from his business in Chandigarh, and soon after permanently succumbed to the call of his lifelong passion.

And so it was that he once again commenced his sports career in 2002 and ever since has been a regular entrant at the Chandigarh's Masters Athletics Meet. At the age of sixty-six, he bagged his first gold medal in the 'Above Sixty-five-year-Old' category in long jump at the Connecticut Athlete Meet held at Hartford, USA.

In 2006, when he had turned sixty-eight, he enticed the crowds at the track and field games in Mesa, Arizona, by winning one gold and four silver medals. The journey continued and the world began talking about his achievements. When Gurdev was seventy, he won seven gold medals in 100 metres, 200 metres and long jump events in Singapore. Later, during the Malaysian Masters Athletics Meet, where he was enrolled in the 75-79 age category, he won a gold medal in the 100 metre and 200-metre sprints, and also a silver medal at the shotput event. During this time, he also won a gold medal in long jump in Canada. By completing the 60-metres dash in 10.22 seconds in the World Masters Athletics Championship held in Poland for the eighty-plus age group, Gurdev has achieved the top spot in the whole of Asia.

> **Miri-Piri**
> Gurdev wears his full white beard with grace and dons a turban even while running on the field. 'Fitness For Life' is his motto. Besides, he has been a fitness freak all through his life and is focused on nutritional facts rather than gorging on unhealthy food. His aim is to set up a sports complex where the youth of our country would be trained physically as well as undergo psychological counselling whenever needed. He believes in practising *Miri* and *Piri* introduced by the sixth Sikh Guru, Sri Guru Hargobind Sahib. *Miri* refers to governorship and material power, and *Piri* represents spirituality. According to Gurdev, physical training provides material power to a sportsperson and *Piri* aids in improving mental stamina.

His athletic career gave him the opportunity to explore the world and meet people across the globe. He repeatedly qualified and competed in the World Masters Games (an event for older athletes) and he was fascinated by older women taking part in different sporting events. In 2008, while he was participating in the World Masters Games in Canada, he witnessed a ninety-year-old woman participating in the 100-metre lap. This was the first time he got the idea of introducing his mother to sports. Later in 2009, in Australia, he met Olga Kotelko, a nonagenarian track-and-field athlete who had won over 750 gold medals in her age category and held over thirty world records in the Masters competitions. At the World Masters Athletics Championships, she was a sprinter, long jumper, triple jumper, and a high jumper. His mind was made up and he was determined to introduce his own mother to the athletics arena.

'My mother never took medicines or visited doctors. She had no joint or knee ailments. So, I decided to train her for the track and field games,' he said.

However, he was yet to introduce the main player—his mother—to what he proposed to do. Gurdev took a deep breath and began to narrate the whole scenario he had encountered at the World Masters Games and described them to his mother in vivid detail. He was disappointed at first and did not receive any enthusiastic response! He decided to give her time to get familiar with the idea. Would she ever be ready to participate?

How You Can Get Rid of Restlessness
- The move to a new city made Maan restless as she yearned to get back to work. So, the first step will be to identity the cause of your restlessness.
- Share with your children or friends—trust them and give them a chance to understand your situation. Even oldies need a push!
- Do not be shy to advertise your novel work to your friends and neighbours.

- Hard work never goes in vain so keep working to evade restlessness. Work had been a constant element in Maan's life, and proved to be her sole saviour.
- Sometimes, an idea works like a catalyst, like Olga's example motivated Maan.
- Restlessness pushed Maan to bring a revolutionary change into her life!

Chapter 6

GOD PROPOSES, WO-MAAN RUNS!

Bereavement struck when Maan's husband passed away. It was as if the very purpose of her existence was wiped out. It affected her health. All those years in Chandigarh, she had kept a busy schedule accommodating both her profitable hobbies and balancing them with her family responsibilities. She had never missed cooking her husband's favourite meals or putting his desires ahead of her own. She had looked after him with utmost care and affection and had dedicated her life to the service of the 102-year-old, Ranjit Singh. Accepting his inevitable demise was the only solution to cope with this sudden change that had come in her life. She was engulfed by a feeling of emptiness and grief, and she knew that she had to find a way to live with this loss. Again, she found solace in the art of sewing and this went a long way in helping to mend her soul.

Maan was still recovering from this first wound, when she felt further isolated when her second son chose to live independently. For an Indian family living in the same city, making a choice to live separately and thereby moving away from the joint family system is still not so common. It took time, but eventually she relented and accepted the fact. Confronting both these truths helped her to recover from the trauma caused by her son's departure and from the loss of her companion. Everything seemed to have happened at once, and Maan felt the pain of separation from her son was deeper than the trauma she had experienced when losing her own mother during her birth.

The onus fell on Gurdev to help his mother deal with this sudden misery. In the same year, Gurdev too had lost his wife, who had just turned sixty a few days before her death. He himself was grieving over the loss of his wife and father, and as the eldest son, he believed that it was his duty to take care of his mother. Suddenly, after the demise of Gurdev's wife, Maan was left with just one member in the house and regretted not valuing the days when her daughter-in-law was around and bestowing her with more affection. She missed the times when her home was filled with the hustle and bustle of her grandchildren, daughters-in-law, and the demanding voice of her husband.

Choosing to Move On
Maan could not change what had happened, but she

could accept and surrender to her fate. She knew that when she would do this, her wounds would eventually heal over time. She realised that shadows are a consequence of sunlight, but believed that altering her direction in life was in her hands. And so, she chose to gaze at the sun!

During this period, Gurdev once again narrated the story of Olga Kotelko to his extremely depressed mother. He knew the only way for his mother to regain her old cheerful nature was to pull herself out of her seclusion and set a goal for herself in life. It took days for Gurdev to persuade his mother to fill the empty space with a new challenge. Although Maan resisted at first, she was soon convinced by Gurdev.

A Divine Proposal Welcomed by Maan

A centenarian without any chronic diseases, disability or cognitive impairment was nature's god-sent gift for her athletic career. Her temple-like body not only offered her physical strength, but also helped in developing a powerful mindset. She had never run before, but her exceptional longevity owing to her disease-free body was her greatest asset. She now needed to push her limits and train as a runner. This was almost like a divine proposal, one that she readily accepted. She regarded this as a *Hukam* of the Almighty.

Maan, who was just four-foot-eleven inches tall and weighed just forty-seven kilograms, had no idea that she was a natural athlete and had tons of talent packed in her small frame. Fear of the unknown had never dampened her elated spirit. With the keenness to explore and learn new things, she flagged off this journey with her son. The casual morning walks helped in the initial training. She simply maintained that pace and never hurried to prove anything to the world. Once again, fun and excitement came her way! These were her new companions, along with her trainer son.

Being an athlete himself, Gurdev very well knew the difference between a sprinter and a marathon runner. Sprinting is a game of a few seconds, while the other one endures for hours. For this reason, her son took the lead to decide on Maan's genre. Assessing his mother's vigour and considering the benefits of running in older adults, he thought she would excel in sprinting.

Gurdev introduced his mother to the grounds of Panjab University, Chandigarh. She had fond memories of her early training days in this capital city of the two north Indian states of Punjab and Haryana. Maan soon began to enjoy the whole training process. It was like a new adventure for her, a platform in which she could express her childlike innocence. There was an urge to extend the training boundaries set by her son—and she often did what she thought best. It was difficult for Gurdev to restrain his mother's free-spirited soul. She would run independently of her octogenarian son and aim to pack in a few miles extra into her routine. She would not easily accept failure, a self-developed trait in her earlier years. She was ever willing to work upon her shortcomings, and perhaps it was this single-minded devotion to her training that helped her shatter so many world records later.

So far, Maan had led a quiet householder's life. She would pray regularly expressing gratitude to the Almighty, both silently and verbally, admiring nature and spending her time amidst trees, and watching the countless miracles all around her even while performing her regular duties and chores at home. She would often share her earnings with the destitutes she would meet on the roads while on her runs and walks.

> **Sarbat Da Bhala**
> Maan started with a traditional pair of walking shoes as she had no extravagant preferences. She would keep her needs to the bare minimum to liberate her mind from misleading and distracting thoughts of the world and chose instead to focus on her karma. She asked for abundant blessings for the well-being of the whole human race in her daily prayers, and wanted *Sarbat da bhala* or well-being and blessings for everyone. The term describes the Sikh principles and is central to Sikhism, the religion Maan followed.

Followers of the religious philosophy taught by Sri Guru Nanak Dev ji in the fifteenth century call themselves Sikhs. It is among the world's more recent religions, and its scriptures are enclosed in a volume of 1,430 *Ang* or pages called the *Sri Guru Granth Sahib ji*. Following her Sikh tradition, Maan hoped to connect and draw a link with the divine rather than aspiring to merge with the Supreme Power; amalgamation with the creator is peripheral to Sikh theology, Maan believed.

While practising on the ground, she was always worried about our Planet Earth that had to bear her burden of 47 kilograms! She would chant the following verse from the *Jap Ji Sahib*—the first morning prayer of the Sikhs composed by Sri Guru Nanak Dev:

Dharatī Hōr Parai Hōr Hōr
Tis Tē Bhār Talai Kavan Jōr[1]

Translated, this means that there are so many worlds beyond this earth and there are so many countless planets; what then is the power that holds the weight of all these worlds? She staunchly believed that this earth is pure and would fail to carry the burden of evil deeds. Compassion holds the earth and all the myriad worlds in place! Maan would often indulge in self-talk. She would say that it helped bring clarity to her thoughts; this was important when she was about to make decisions. Moreover, she claimed that it helped her touch base with her consciousness and made it easy for her to accept personal or professional defeat in life.

Chapter 7

ONE STEP AT A TIME

The concept of self-owned cars was new for the people of her times and no one looked upon this as an inconvenience. In her self-propelled lifestyle, owning a vehicle was seen as a symbol of luxury rather than a necessity. Public transport was not efficient either, so people used bicycles for offices and families walked to the markets together, while children usually walked to school. Even after carrying out her regular tedious household chores, Maan would be walking to the grocery store and carry rations and groceries on her shoulders. This walking practice now stood her in good stead and turned out to be a blessing in disguise. She brought all the household goods and cooking materials from the market. Maan was like the proverbial delivery girl for the family. Her mother would ask to run all her little errands and Maan would sometimes end up taking several rounds of the local stores. She was instructed by her father to fetch things for her grandmother, and she happily did all this.

Hence, Maan was used to walking and this helped her in the sports world. Her walking partner, Gurdev, enjoyed strolling around with his mother in the parks of Chandigarh and also served as her specialised track and field coach. She would mostly use the Panjab University campus as her training ground, but to add excitement in the formative years of her career, Gurdev included walking around Chandigarh's popular Sukhna Lake as a part of her casual training. To keep his mother's interest alive in these often, daily monotonous walking routines, he ensured that he introduced new routes every week. Maan was lucky that she was in Chandigarh, a well-planned city which offered a park in every sector, so they often moved from one sector to another starting from sector 1 to sector 17. Maan was allowed to speak only when they changed from one sector to another! She would then share her feelings and stories that her mind would think of throughout the journey. He marked her progress as she moved through the connecting parks of the sectors. In between, they would trot along on the pavements that were lined by trees on both sides creating beautiful canopies. She would pinpoint a new tree every day and weave a story around these trees. The result was that Maan enjoyed her daily outings-cum-practice sessions.

To keep up the tempo and to increase his mother's

enthusiasm in sports, Gurdev had initiated her into these easy, recreational walks. These helped Maan develop the right mindset necessary for entering the competitive field. Gurdev had to now turn his mother's focus towards medal-winning by taking part in the National Senior Games!

> **Can a Centenarian Learn to Compete at the World Level?**
> Competing at the National Senior Games was a giant leap for which Maan needed time. Gurdev developed a comprehensive training programme for her, focusing not just on physical training but also placing equal emphasis on developing her skill and stamina. He needed to bring her up to speed so that she could compete at the world level. Gurdev worked on her, educationally, mentally, and physically. He made sure his mother was updated with contemporary knowledge of the world. He was seventy when he trained himself to serve as a model coach and an instructor to his mother. Apart from this, she had her faith and her belief in her Creator to propel her along towards victory. Maan had started step by step and relied on her willpower to move forward. She believed the entire cosmos walked with her—in every single step that she took!

Chapter 8

HOLLOW BONES AND A FRESH START

Maan and Gurdev then took a decision to move back to her place of birth and hometown, Patiala. Maharani Preneet Kaur served as a minister of state in the Ministry of External Affairs from 2009-14. Her husband is Captain Amarinder Singh, the son and heir of the Maharaja of Patiala and the 26th Chief Minister of Punjab. Preneet Kaur supported Maan's stay in the city and welcomed her back to Patiala. Gurdev eagerly seized this patronage from the politician, with both hands!

Thus, Maan and Gurdev were allotted free accommodation in the lush green campus of the Punjabi University, Patiala. It is a university that has been awarded 'Five-star' and 'A+' grade by the National Assessment and Accreditation Council (NAAC).[1] The standard athletics cinder track of 400 metres and IAAF (International Association of Athletic Federations) synthetic athletics track of Punjabi University gave her the right platform for training to compete at international levels. Maan was both pleased and relieved to have this accommodation near her training ground.

The head of the sports department conducted a full body test on Maan. The reports baffled the staff and professors, who were with Maan throughout her physical examination. They were all there to support her, and everyone was surprised when an X-ray of her spinal cord showed a shocking picture. Maan was diagnosed with a C-shaped lumbar scoliosis, a condition which causes discomfort while walking or even standing. And here was this miracle woman who was courageously competing in track-and-field events, winning them and shattering world records! For doctors, this condition defied explanation.

Older people, above the age of fifty, are usually affected by this disease and she was exactly double that age when she was tested at the Bhai Ghaniya Health Centre in the Punjabi University campus in 2017. At 101, she defied all the medical theories advocating precautions and treatment options for a person with scoliosis.

'Her spine indicates the hard slog of her times,' a medical examiner exclaimed while scanning her X-ray. Performing multiple jobs such as milling, spinning, sewing, weaving, and knitting can often be a cause for that curve in the spine. However, this did not stop Maan from doing all those jobs. She went on to break records at the World Masters Games, that too with a C-shaped lumbar—this was another miracle that mystified her doctors. Maan's spine was healing naturally without any medicines or precautions. By the age of 103, her body was showing advance signs of self-healing!

> **When it's Healthy to Shun Your Doctor's Prescription!**
> Maan had lived life on her own terms, without obsessing over the prescribed preventive care and guidelines laid down by her doctors. Physicians wouldn't ever have allowed such a person to slouch over an object or run on the track field, but Maan did all of that and excelled at them, too, despite being a centenarian. Warm-up exercises that included stretching coupled with her training regimen were healing her body. It helped her muscles to loosen up and counter whatever deterioration they would have otherwise undergone over time.

In the wildest of her dreams, Maan had never thought that she would train in the competitive sports arena! Accompanying her son Gurdev, for morning park walks was all that Maan had in her sports' bucket list. She was ninety-three when her son had come up with this novel idea and she had started to train at an age which most people do not ever even reach. Soon after her debut, she proudly reported her first sporting event to her fans! She gave full credit to her son for motivating her to take up sports and said that this fact changed her life, both physically and mentally. She cheerfully asserted, '*Mere jeevan da ae sabto sohna waqt hai!*' — 'I am having the best time of my life!'

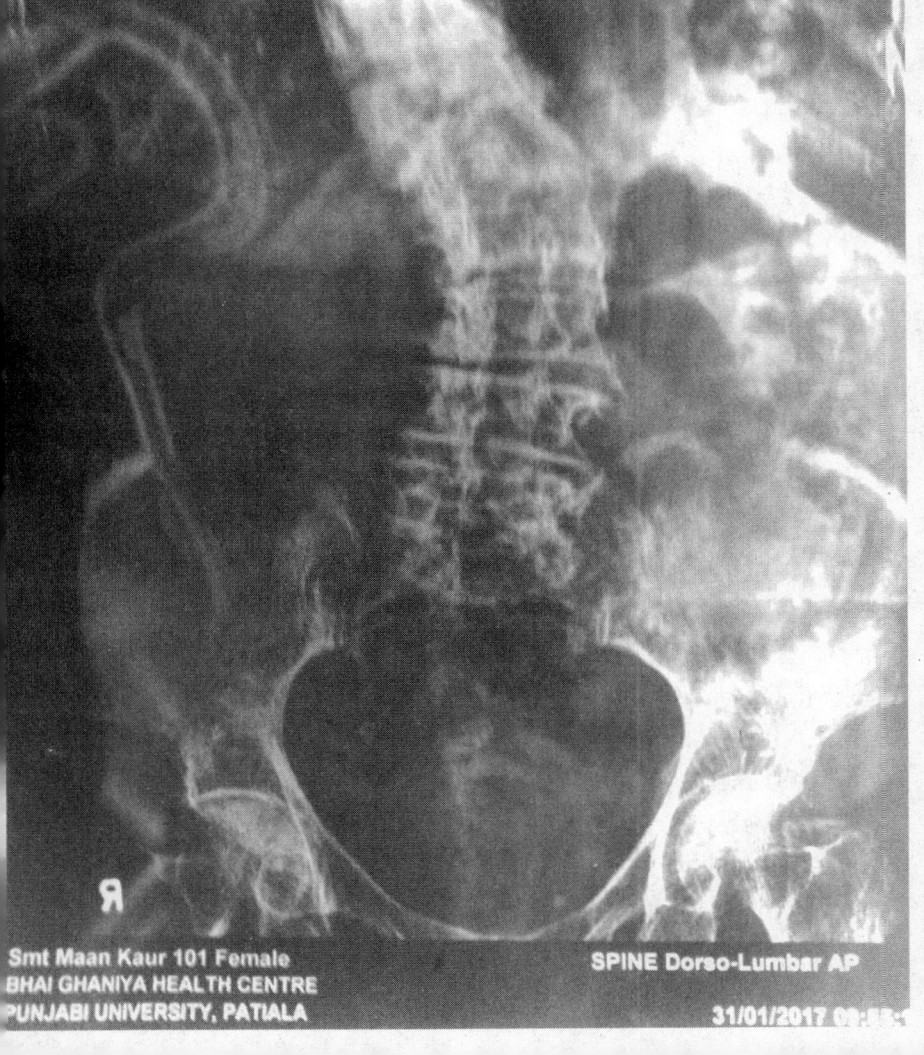

Chapter 9

A NOVEL EXPERIMENT

The sports trials at Patiala University proved to be a huge success for Maan. This was just the beginning of a novel experiment conducted on her which helped to renew hope in a ninety-three-year-old loner. The seed of the experiment that was sown to counter isolation finally matured at the 32nd National Masters Athletics Championships in Chandigarh. This was the platform where Maan was identified as a budding athlete. It marked a turning point in her life.

The National Masters Athletics for veterans, especially for newcomers, was a gift that she received when she was well into her nineties. Maan won the gold medal in the 100 metres and 200 metres in the ninety-plus category, and this victory at the national level in Chandigarh qualified her to participate in the World Masters Athletics (WMA) meet. She was now perfectly trained for clearing the entry level requirements in the WMA. All these years of dedicated practice helped Maan build her stamina and improve her concentration levels. After analysing his mother's performance, and thoroughly studying the hundred-page long technical rules for participating in the international games, Gurdev saw a bright future ahead for his mother in athletics.

Henceforth, a comprehensive road map was prepared by Gurdev which she executed by participating in all the national and international level games for senior citizens. Despite her growing age, Maan's determination and passion for participating in competitive games kept increasing, and gradually, she began to enjoy the exposure and media attention that was now coming her way. Maan continued to impress with her performances till her last breath.

> **Overcoming Criticism**
> It is not as if Maan did not receive her share of criticism, but she overcame that with her patience, a vital trait in handling criticism that is inevitable in the life of a successful sportsperson. Harsh words and criticism did not provoke shame, fear or anger within her. Instead, she remained calm and collected, then understood and examined what was being said of her. She was ambitious and her desire to acquire more and more trophies egged her on to achieve more.

Maan was now open to interact with world-class elite performers and this motivated her to stick to the new adventure she had been introduced to. She was entirely unaware that she was about to join the elite league of legendary figures like Fauja Singh, John Whittemore, Herman Smith-Johannsen, Ruth Frith, Everett Hosack and other record-breaking centenarians. Though Maan had known Fauja Singh personally, she was oblivious of the foreign track and athletics superstars.

Gurdev had personally raced with Fauja Singh in an International Marathon from Chamkaur Sahib to Fatehgarh Sahib that had been organised by the Punjab Government in 2004, around the time when Gurdev first began toying with the idea of transforming his mother's life. A healthy body, which is crucial and central to earn success in this field had given wings to his idea.

'Physical function is the most important factor that contributes to healthy ageing and all the centenarian celebrities had this in common. My mother too falls into this category of age-defying seniors,' Gurdev had said back then.

> **The Importance of Physical Movement**
> Regular, physical movement while doing regular chores around the house has been scientifically associated with wellbeing and fitness among the older population.[1]
> There was no programmed list of actions that Maan had

> followed while she was ageing. But she had continued being physically active. It was all thanks to her heavy-duty traditional Indian kitchen implements that have disappeared from modern kitchens that had kept Maan strong, apart from the regular walking she did to complete her chores.

These actions had prepared Maan for competitions. She had held on to her traditional methods of cooking and was always dead against modern twenty-first century mechanised equipment and appliances. To the people of today, she might seem rooted in old, traditional methods of chopping, cutting, cooking and grinding on a slab and stone, but she had resisted modern cooking aids for a reason. She knew very well the side-effects of a microwave and was aware of its harmful radiation that caused loss of nutrients in food cooked or warmed in it. So, she did not permit Gurdev to bring modern equipment into her kitchen. She equally opposed air fryers and dishwashers as the extra energy and water consumed by some of these appliances was a matter of concern. When people suggested she install a chimney, she said she would not have this noisy machine and would much rather prefer to keep her big kitchen window wide open to get rid of the smoke!

'These machines are making our human race lazy, and we might lose our motor ability one day, because of them,' she would say.

Want to Become Extraordinary?

With conscious living and continuous training of mind and body, Maan had the perfect formula that enabled her to live a balanced and disease-free life. She became a role model and a living example of how the right attitude towards life can contribute to physical health. She raised the bar and demolished all negative stereotypes related to old age. Maan, didn't discover her talent just by chance. Instead, she made sure that she excelled because of the intense hard work and research that she put into this. She paid detailed attention to her training routine and made sure to protect herself from diseases like widespread arrhythmia ailment in athletes and in sprinters, cyclists, and among participants of high-paced events.[2] After a session she would regularly check her heartbeat as soon as she got home.

Maan's Way:
1. Conscious living and positive attitude towards life.
2. Continuous training of mind and body.
3. Demolish negative stereotypes.
4. Know that nothing happens by chance; put in effort to achieve your goals.
5. Be attentive and protect yourself from mental and physical degradation.
6. Be your own examiner.

Chapter 10

THE FIRST RUN

Maan was reassured about her perfect athletic skills when she tasted success at the first national run. This was when Gurdev shared more plans with his mother about her future as a runner. Over the past few years, his mind had been actively framing a future timetable for her at international events. This exciting plan helped to give him a goal as well as overcome and reduce his own stress levels. He knew his mother had the makings of a winner and he also knew that this target could be easily achieved with the help of consistent training. His desire to see his mother as a sportsperson was to give her life a purpose—but this eventually turned out to be a huge international celebration and success story.

The novel experiment in Chandigarh led to rigorous and serious training back home on the campus of the Punjabi University. Maan had just turned ninety-five and was prepared to overcome all limitations that age may have set for her besides redefining the Indian mindset related to older folk. Maan put down her resilience to having been born at a tough time and having experienced first-hand the orthodox culture of the 1930s as well as being witness to the present times where women have the freedom to choose what they wanted to do. She was, therefore, all set and ready to prepare for her new role; her physical body and mental ability helped her to become an award-winning centenarian-runner and athlete.

Maan now began preparing for the upcoming World Masters Athletics Championships, scheduled to be held in the United States of America. The training regime for a ninety-five-year-old protégé had to be extremely sophisticated and well-designed. Her son decided to change her training pattern and customise her freestyle exercises keeping in mind that she was now two years older. He began reading and referring to the training plans of centenarians across the globe, but he also knew that starting her off on an aggressive training could prove harmful. For this reason, he avoided sudden, unplanned exercises. He was also aware of his mother's extraordinary abilities and was in no hurry to prove them to the world. By the time, a person advances into the nineties, it is a known fact that they lose a tremendous amount of muscle mass and that their ability to live a fast-paced life is reduced by almost 50 per cent.[1] But she was born different. And

Gurdev knew that it was up to him alone to channelise Maan's potential so that she could achieve the unexpected.

But the biggest challenge that Gurdev faced while imparting training lessons to Maan was managing her free-spirited soul. He began by explaining the relevance of warm-up exercises just before and after the end of each training session, but that was like opening a pandora's box! A heap of emotions would take over Maan when she began her stretches and warm-up exercises and she would want to perform much more than what had been specified by Gurdev. This rebellious mindset brought trouble to Maan and resulted in physical issues. Consequently, Gurdev would not leave his mother alone during her training sessions. He would stand beside her and guide the pace of each of her steps to keep a check on how much she was exercising.

> **A Childlike Approach to Life**
> Many believe that it was Maan's never-say-die spirit that led her to achieve so much! Her childlike approach to life did not allow age to come in the way of her exploring, experimenting, and learning something new each day, along with the rising sun.

By now, she knew every inch of her training terrain—its structure, area, and shape, the ground surfaces, oval and straight tracks. She learned about track markings and about the relevance of the white lanes in athletic games. By and large, Gurdev had been successful in providing a well-rounded training to his mother and as a result, she could literally measure her progress on the ground, inch by inch.

At first, it was a guided run, and she would sprint without really understanding her true objective for running or what it was that she had to achieve, but with regular training, she was finally able to identify the scope of track and field games. Later, Maan could easily spot the targets that she would conquer each day. During her practice sessions, she also began planning her next move on the ground with her coach son, Gurdev. In all her competitions, Gurdev would take the responsibility for the start lines. But what attracted Maan the most was the finish line!

By then, Maan had learned what it meant when people talked about the anaerobic temperament of sprint events, and she became conscious of the speed that she should not cross and the rules that were not supposed to be broken. Training gave her running a certain finesse, but she was still driven by her free-spirited nature which told her that she must follow her heart more than rules.

Soon it was time to head overseas for her first international event. Maan was excited to cross the international borders for the first time in her life. Gurdev was understandably apprehensive and had mixed feelings of happiness, nervousness and also of the unknown. He had no idea how his mother would face the long flight.

By the time I had met Maan, she had given repeated and detailed accounts of her first international trip to several friends, relatives, acquaintances and interviewers. She told me that when it was finally time for her first journey, she had gotten rid of her fears, doubts and apprehensions and had decided to embrace her first new journey like an infant who is ready for every new experience and adventure without a single thought of the consequences. Maan with all her enthusiasm, was all set to dive right in. All she knew was that she was heading outside *Bharat's* borders.

The World Masters Athletics (WMA) Championships at Sacramento, in the United States of America, was her first international tournament. She participated in the track and field events with a fair amount of ease. But breaking the psychological barrier of seeing so many foreign spectators proved a little unnerving for Maan. She could feel a storm of negative emotions attacking her when she took her first foot forward in this foreign land. Fortunately, she did not understand the language and thus, had no idea whether she was being praised or criticised. Thus, her innocence proved a boon. However, Gurdev's anxiety increased, and he felt obliged to prove to the world that his mother was capable of winning.

The spectators looked at her disbelievingly, thinking of how this short, old lady could even complete the race! Her first event was a 100-metre dash followed by a 200-metre race. It was Gurdev who guided Maan to take off at the sound of the starting pistol as she could not understand the motive behind a blank gunshot. She described that first experience:

'*Pataka vajya hor main oo gayi.*'— 'I heard a loud bang and I started to run.'

This was the track and field event where she not only won two gold medals, both in the 100 metre and 200 metre races but was also declared Athlete of the Year, 2011.

From here on, her journey of breaking world records flagged off. The camaraderie that followed after the Masters Games built her confidence, and she gradually started looking forward to participating at these events.

Chapter 11

OUT OF PATIALA

Patiala was the only world Maan knew till her husband got a transfer and moved to Chandigarh. But even then, she had never moved out beyond India's northern region. Life can be full of surprises and she was often amazed at the all-new world she discovered when she was well into her nineties. She believed this to be the second innings of her life in which she got an opportunity to travel almost the whole world—not as a tourist, but as a sports celebrity.

Maan had been on several train journeys while travelling to Chail and accompanying the Ranis of Maharaja Bhupinder Singh. But the move from the trains of the quaint old Indian Railway to swanky, international airports was a journey she had never imagined. Ever willing to drink in new experiences, she observed everything at the airports. She had expected something like a railway station and was startled to see the dazzling lights which made even night feel like a bright day. She was absolutely mesmerised but was ready to soak in this novel experience. Watching the luggage on the conveyor belts and aircraft parked around in the hangars amused her. The take-off experience in the aircraft felt as if she was on a giant seesaw.

'*Jahaz kade hetha nu hove kade upar nu jave,*' she said to me, while describing her experience of a flight. Translated, her sentence means, 'Sometimes the airplane went up and sometimes down.'

She maintained her poise while looking around at her co-passengers. Now that she was firmly ensconced in her seat, she stared out of the window for a clearer view of the other aircraft on the tarmac but once high above the ground, the myriad shapes of the clouds blew her imagination. Everything was going smoothly and she was busy taking in the window view, when her ear's eustachian tubes suddenly seemed to be giving her trouble. Gurdev, her very own superhero-son, was literally on his toes anticipating what could go wrong. This happened just at the beginning of the world tours. The issues detected in the first round of air travel were taken care of in the subsequent journeys. Earplugs worked best for Maan to prevent clogging due to unequal air pressure on the two sides of the ear drum.

Half the battle was won for Gurdev when he realised that a positive flight, without any untoward incident helped his mother drop future travel insecurities. A comfortable flight meant that his mother was ready to hit the tracks after resting to take care of jet lag. Once she had adjusted to air travel, he was confident that she was ready for the long haul and would return home a winner at the age of ninety-five, breaking old traditions and taking up new challenges in foreign countries, when a majority of folks at her age are confined to their *charpai* or bed, simply awaiting their end.

Gurdev had already warned me: 'Do not undermine my mother's memory!'

Even at the age of 105, no one could challenge her prefrontal cortex. She could as easily commit short-term events to memory as well as narrate long-forgotten stories from her life with ease. Faces and experiences of the past remained fresh and vivid in her mind. When asked about what was the secret behind her sprightly and ever-active personality, her tireless energy and strength, she offered some ageless wisdom in her simple answer:

'Guru dainda hai shakti. Main ni boldi, Guru ji bolwande ne.' She said that her Creator gives her strength. She added, 'I am not saying this; it is my Lord who makes me say these words.'

Most people are hesitant to leave the comfort zone of their own home and you can imagine how Maan at the age of ninety-five was ready to not just travel, but also take part as a sprinter, running in a foreign land in an unfamiliar stadium and on an unknown track.

Moreover, certain norms had to be followed and the most challenging was her attire. Till this point, Gurdev had thought that moving 'out of Patiala' was among Maan's biggest challenge. Now came the real test; not only was she in a foreign land, but he now had to ask his mother to modify her outfit for the competitions and get out of her customary Patiala salwars and kameez.

Since her birth, the only dress she had adored and was comfortable in was her Patiala salwars and Maan continued abiding by the traditional dress code set by her ancestors. Initially, for events back in India, she substituted the kameez with a loose T-shirt as the length of the usual kameez interfered and prevented smooth performance and movement, but Maan continued wearing her two metre-wide salwar, and she refused to alter her authentic Patiala attire, till she was due to participate in the American Athletics Championships. Gradually, she was convinced and accepted that she would have to forgo this traditional outfit and shift completely to a sports tracksuit.

Once again, Gurdev had to make the first move and gently suggest a change and then help her acclimatise to the new outfit. Initially, she resisted wearing the tracksuit, specifically track pants on the training grounds. For almost a century, Maan had not worn anything else and Gurdev knew this old habit and lifestyle would be tough to break. So, Gurdev would give his mother the liberty to wear her traditional salwars every alternate day, till she herself realised how adversely it affected her performance. She would also carry a *dupatta* that was two and a half meters long and would drape it over her shoulders! She would even wear this on top of her tracksuit. On his mother's insistence, Gurdev reluctantly agreed to this, but only allowed it during practice sessions.

While participating in competitions, she would skip the dupatta, but flatly refused to take off her *dastar* (head cover) and no one could ever force her to run or appear in public without a black cover on her head. She was never spotted without her *dastar*. She had it on even at home during mealtimes and even before sleeping. It was a symbol of her high self-esteem, spirituality, and self-respect. That was Maan Kaur for you!

> **Never Forget Your Roots**
> Beyond the borders of Patiala city, many questioned her about the head cover that she would always wear. She would reply in a firm voice, *'Eh thae, Guru da taaz hai'* (This is my Lord's Crown). Until the end of time, Maan wore her headdress, and remained self-motivated to perform, never being overwhelmed by the ethnic and cultural diversity of any of the countries that she would visit around the globe. She retained her individuality and took pleasure in crossing boundaries and creating history by breaking world records.

The WMA Championships at Sacramento, California was just the beginning for the unstoppable lady! Forever after that, the United States of America held a special place in her heart as this was her first and foremost international destination. She often relived that cherished moment by sharing it with her guests, friends and visitors. The Asian Masters Athletics Championships in Taiwan was the next event in which she further proved her mettle. As time progressed, the number of countries she visited increased, along with her ever-increasing age; and yet her performances kept on improving and Maan continued to break her own records. Now that she had toured almost every significant country around the globe, her public exposure and popularity increased. Italy, Vancouver, New Zealand, Spain, Poland, Malaysia, Canada—the list of countries she participated in seemed endless for a 105-year-old great-grandmother!

While competing at all these famous international tracks, she would often repeat a *shlok*—a verse that people of the Sikh faith often repeat:

Pavan Guru Pāṇī Pitā Mātā Dharat Mahat
Divas Rāt Dui Dāī Dāiā Khaylai Sagal Jagat
Changiāīā Buriāīā Vāchai Dharam Hadur
Karamī Āpo Āpaṇī Kay Nayrai Kay Dur
Jinī Nām Dhiāiā Gaay Masakat Ghāl
Nānak Kay Mukh Ujalay Kaytī Chhuṭī Nāl[1]

Guru Nanak, Jap Ji Sahib

Air is the *Guru* (teacher), water is the father and earth is the great Mother of all the grounds on which I run. Day and night are the two nurses, in whose lap I rest after a tiring run. The records of good and bad deeds are read out in the presence of the Lord of Dharma. Based on one's own actions, some are drawn near to God and some are sent far away. There are those who have meditated, worked and departed by the sweat of their brows. O Nanak, their faces are radiant in the Court of the Lord, and many are saved along with them!

Chapter 12

LOVE AND MORE LOVE AT NEW ZEALAND

Maan had just turned 101!
For Gurdev, it was a matter of immense pride that the life of his diminutive-statured mother who was less than five feet tall was large enough to position India on the world map in Senior Games. Maan approached life with the zest and verve of a fluttering butterfly who wanted to pack in as much excitement as was possible in one lifetime. With the special magic that she would weave on the athletics tracks, she could instantly mesmerise a person, and New Zealand could not resist the allure of her charismatic smile. This scenic country of endless beaches, spectacular earth holes, verdant land, snowy peaks, and splendid fjords attracted Maan. Above all, she was touched by the humility of the local people.

It was 2017, time for the World Masters Games to be held in Auckland. Maan had been looking forward to seeing herself race at the age of 101. Accordingly, she spent several months training herself to participate in various track and field events in Auckland. Before every international competition, she had to compete with life's reality, as travelling long distances at that age was tiring and no longer, particularly exciting. But this journey was exceptional, giving her one more reason to be glad that she had found sprinting as her vocation. From the time, Maan and Gurdev boarded the flight, their stay at New Zealand till their return journey, every moment proved special and filled with warm memories.

Before the flight took off, the pilot and crew members surprised her with a cake-cutting ceremony which made Maan feel special. They even sang a selection of Punjabi *Boliyan* and *Tappe* (couplets sung to celebrate special occasions in Punjab) on the flight and Maan accepted this honour, together with Gurdev, gracefully. She participated in the singing and even danced like a teen!

Though it was a long flight, the care that Maan received from the crew members made the journey seem short and enjoyable. She felt like royalty, like Akbar must have felt when he was entertained by Birbal's intriguing stories! No wonder, Maan found life exciting and it reflected in her twinkling, shiny eyes. She cherished love, life and humanity and spread happiness among the people who were around her. She traversed her life's journey based on this principle and received an equal amount of love and compassion in return. She came back with wonderful memories of her stay in New Zealand.

At the airport, Maan was welcomed like a star, and was overwhelmed by the bouquets and support she received. She had no idea about what was awaiting her at Auckland airport and when the flight landed, she spotted a team of press reporters recording her every move, and later, she was guided towards an interview room. She learned that media personnel had arrived long earlier and had waited to take the first look at this 101-year-old track and field icon. The media wanted to know details about the events in which she was going to compete, and, above all, they wanted to speak to Maan about the secret behind her longevity.

To Gurdev's surprise, the president of the World Masters Games was there to receive this puny great-grandmother from India. And this had created a stir and a sizzle among the news reporters. The mother-son duo had been welcomed with garlands and volunteers facilitated their every move. And you bet, Maan was really pleased with this outpouring of love at the airport in a foreign nation. With all the felicitations and positivity that had come her way, Gurdev was sure of his mother's victory at the World Masters Games, 2017. This was the time when he realised that the sports journey that the two had undertaken just a decade earlier had catapulted his mother into the limelight. It was a surreal experience, and he was understandably excited, yet at the same time, he was filled with gratitude.

Maan's participation in the Canadian Masters Athletics Championships and the World Senior Games held in the USA in 2013 had already prepared Maan for the thrill of competing at large-scale events. She had observed at close hand how other players trained and performed at the competitions. The World Masters Games (WMG) are held every four years and are governed by the International Masters Games Association (IMGA). These games are open to all but every competitor must have a minimum age of thirty, barring a few sports that are open only to younger competitors.

The ninth World Masters Games were hosted in Auckland. The legacy of the World Masters Games began in the summer of 1985 when a record 8,305 master athletes gathered in Toronto, Canada, for the first ever World Masters Games.

Expectations from Maan had increased after her record-breaking performance in 2016 at the IMGA-administered Americas Masters Games (AMG). Maan participated in the first edition of these games which had competitions in twenty-four sporting disciplines ranging from archery to volleyball. The AMG have no qualification prerequisites for competing except the minimum age requirement which is also set at thirty. Maan's confidence was high after participating in the AMG at Vancouver, where she had received immense respect from dignitaries and spectators. Maan wanted to go all out and be an example for the youth.

At all international tournaments, doors of the local Sikh gurudwara (temple) were always open for the duo with an offer of free accommodation and meals. This is how the duo managed to participate in so many overseas meets. Moreover, given her lifestyle and culture, she was comfortable staying at the premises of the *Gurudwara Sahib*. In New Zealand, her daily needs of lentils and chapati were met by the community kitchen of the gurudwaras. She certainly would not have been able to adjust to the diet provided by star hotels if she was required to live there.

While at these gurudwaras, she would regularly perform *seva* (voluntary service) by chopping vegetables, washing utensils, and making chapatis for visitors, all through her one-month long stay in Auckland.

To Maan, New Zealand's landscape and foliage was like a sweet lullaby, and she looked forward to her early morning training sessions at Lovelock Track at the Wesley Community Centre in Mount Roskill—and although she did not leave any love locks, the track, nevertheless, romantically connected with her.

During the day, she actively chipped in with chores in the community kitchen. Gurdev monitored her daily activities with the other volunteers of the temple and ensured that his mother rested to her full capacity, so that she was ready for her routine workouts. Maan was, thus, thoroughly prepared to give her best at the games.

Daily transport from the event venue to the Gurudwara Sri Kalgidhar Sahib, Takanini, was arranged by the New Zealand police headquarters for ten consecutive days. People from different walks of life came forward to assist Maan, all of them taken in by her boundless energy. People would flock in to meet her or just be happy to watch her participate at an event. Her presence, itself, was sufficient to create a buzz.

In an interview, Jennah Wootten, the chief executive of the World Masters Games asserted: 'Maan Kaur truly personifies the "Sport for all" philosophy which the World Masters Games is all about and we are thrilled to have her here.'

After her debut in the javelin throw, shot put and 400 metres race in Canada, this time she was prepared to give her best in these track and field events in Auckland. Gurdev was literally like her shadow, gently guiding his mother, all through the events. Maan delivered a world record-breaking performance by winning five gold medals—one each in the 100 metres, 200 metres, 400 metres, javelin throw and shot put. Shot put turned out to be her favourite game and she gleefully told me in Punjabi, *'Is vaari mai fir gola sitiya.'*— 'This time, I again threw the round-shaped ball.'

Maan broke the Javelin Guinness World Record with her 5.12 metres throw at the Trusts Stadium in Waitakere. Post-race, her jaunty victory dance in front of the crowd while flashing peace signs for her fans made her a sensation at the games and this became her most memorable feat. Breaking records seemed fun to the centenarian, and she looked forward to motivating people to strive against life's many vicissitudes.

Their New Zealand trip did not conclude with the World Masters Games. On a whim, Maan wanted to extend her stay for a few more days and the Government of New Zealand was happy to oblige and hosted them with pride. Maan was comfortable walking around and exploring New Zealand. She was spellbound every time with its scenic beauty and its two large, picturesque harbours. She visited Kelly Tarlton's Underwater World, Auckland's War Memorial Museum, Waiheke Island, and some of the exceptional beaches that Auckland city has in abundance. They were also invited to see Auckland's 328 meters-long iconic skyline. She could not believe her luck, when she saw the cliffs rising from the fjords and waterfalls of Maori Aotearoa—all of this had existed so far, only in a fantasy world of fairytales.

Apart from her sporting feats, she became the oldest woman in the world to walk the Sky Tower's skyline. In no time, she slipped into a vibrant orange jumpsuit, even though it was a size too big for her. Safety rules were detailed to Maan before she could capture an 80-kilometre-wide view of the city walking at a height of 192 metres! Fastening a set of harnesses onto her, the staff on duty at the Sky Tower warned Maan not to look downwards or lean over the edge, but while walking, she was too thrilled to remember the guidelines. She said to the instructor, that 'looking at my age, one should neither be hyper-cautious nor alter the rules!' After strapping more safety gear onto her, the staff understood the importance of what she was trying to tell them when they saw her holding her son's hand and confidently taking the lead while still following the few necessary instructions. Then, compelled by her nature, she merrily looked down to view the world from that enormous height from where buildings resembled tiny Lego houses. She simply chose to do things according to her instincts—it seemed that adrenaline rushes were something that came naturally to her!

The Sugar Club hosted Maan and Gurdev for lunch where they relished both the delicacies and the incredible 360-degree view of the city. Maan described this once-in-a-lifetime experience with me with a gleam in her eyes and joyfully described having food at the top of the Sky Tower. Being a hardcore vegetarian, Maan remembered that she and her son relished pumpkin soup with some vegetables, risotto, and berries. Apart from food, she filled her lungs with the clean and pollution-free air of the city, and stuffed some great memories into her mind's eye to carry back to India.

Fit Body, Healthy Mind

While exploring the city to her heart's content, she asked Gurdev if it was possible to organise a few social activities in the city. Within the premises of the *Gurudwara Sahib,* the duo gave talks encouraging people to take up sports, and to include physical activity for a fit body and more importantly, a healthy mind! They visited schools and institutions training young minds to achieve their life's goals. Maan's advice to the youth was to focus, and thereby progress and climb the ladder of success. She emphasised on the positive influence that regular physical movement can have on the academic and social lives of children. The duo also stressed the relevance of following a sensible, nutritious diet plan and how good food and a matching physical routine could benefit them. She held a special session for the parents of these children and encouraged them to set fitness goals for their families.

Maan inspired the youth by sharing lifestyle tips and told them that following in her footsteps would help them avoid health complications such as diabetes, cardiovascular diseases, and arthritis. She elaborated on the major dietary changes that her own son had made her follow. She gave several interviews through the media to reach a wider audience. She also regaled them with stories about her early, formative years, detailing the basic standard of living of her times.

The extended sojourn in Auckland passed surprisingly quickly, and she found it difficult to leave this island nation. Eventually, it was time for goodbyes and many people came to meet Maan for the last time. She was recognised by the New Zealand Police force for competing in 'The World Masters Games' and they presented a memento with her name embossed on it. Around a hundred people gathered at the ceremony to celebrate Maan's achievements, and to celebrate her unusual life.

She was overwhelmed with this outpouring of love and the crowd applauded in appreciation. Apart from the awards, what moved Maan the most were the gifts of affection that she received—from the inquiry officer, the gym instructor, and from people who had gathered there to bid her adieu. She felt blessed to be a participant at the World Masters Games in Auckland. Maan never expected that her walks and runs would take her all the way from Patiala to New Zealand!

Chapter 13

DIGDI HAAN,
TE JITDI HAAN—I FALL, SO I WIN!

Empathy played a critical role in Maan's life; she could selflessly love, connect with the world and emphasise on universal brotherhood purely because of the monotheistic Sikhism faith she believed in. The only true relationship that filled the emptiness and gaps in her early associations was the one she shared with the Creator. Surrendering her problems and difficulties to the Guru, her spiritual guides helped her overcome her insecurities. Maan was a true seeker, and her spiritual quest began when she was ten, when out of fear, she uttered that magical word, '*Waheguru*', which means, 'Wonderful Lord'![1]

Around the same time, she began speaking to her mother in her dreams. She could delineate her departed mother's facial features and lucidly described her: '*Meri maa bahut sohni si,*' implying that her mother was incredibly beautiful. Nevertheless, she passed this disturbing phase of her life by entering the Lord's court of divinity. Regular practice of this supreme way of life gave solace to her and laid the foundation of her life's philosophy.

Her difficult and sad early childhood years taught her how to rise after every fall. The scoldings of her father and later, the harsh words of her husband made her mind strong enough to bear even physical pain, so she was always prepared for ups and downs in her life, even as a centenarian. Maan had however overcome this by living an adventurous life; Gurdev knew his mother would not settle for a placid, calm life as it simply was not in consonance with her mystical, ever youthful heart.

Maan gave credit for her holistic growth to her grandmother's bedtime stories that were based on parables and contained powerful messages. Maan had a stock of such tales and she took pleasure in narrating a couple of them to her visitors. She could narrate a story for every situation. Her favourite theme stories would highlight the proverb, 'A bird in the hand is worth two in the bush.' Being fond of *karah prasad,* a sweet dish made up of whole wheat, sugar, and clarified butter '*ghee*' mixed in equal portions and distributed in the Sikh gurudwara, Maan would often try her best to get a second helping. She related a specific incident when she tried to hide the *prasad* she had been served in one hand so that she could receive more in the second, but it was all in vain, because it turned out to be a dessert for a dog who was lurking at her feet and who grabbed the 'opportunity' from behind. Meanwhile, the entire *prasad* had already been distributed to the congregation and she ended up getting nothing at all. That day, she decided to take pleasure in what she already owned rather than seeking more.

She could reflect philosophically on every setback, whether it was as inconsequential as her quest for more prasad or the big ones that she encountered later in her life. She learnt invaluable lessons from every one of them.

Prior to every gold medal that Maan had won, she would inadvertently fall down while running, but she would always get up and continue running!

Smilingly, she observed, '*Digdi haan, ta jitdi haan*'— 'I fall, so I win.'

Falling ahead of every competition became her lucky charm! Her countless falls never ever blocked her road to success, and it was because of this that the graph of her life showed an upward trend, despite a few random fluctuations. While competing in the track and field games in Delhi, she experienced her first fall on the competitive track. The response from the spectators was astonishing. None believed that she could ever regain her posture. She suffered a severe back injury once and doctors asked her to quit running. This upset Gurdev, her coach-son who was scared that his happy-go-lucky mother could suffer from some long-term ailments if she continued running.

But despite the pain, and even in the midst of her

treatment, Maan had just said one word to say—'*Daurangi,*' or 'I will run!' And that was that!

Just before she was due to participate in the World Masters Athletics Championships in America, the unfortunate episode occurred for a second time—this time, the fall was far graver than her last one. Maan suffered a head and neck trauma, which was perceived to be a fracture. Instantly, her pulse rate had risen and blood flow to the brain had ceased and doctors forbade Maan to go ahead with the competition. However, Gurdev did not pay much attention to this and waited to see how Maan would react. She would definitely not give up, he thought. A myriad emotions flooded Maan's mind when she heard the doctors' warnings. But even this incident failed to shake her resolve. She took first-aid and stood up once again to participate in the meet. From here on, Gurdev learned to take these emotional rollercoasters in his stride—these only signified his mother's resolve and resilience. Despite all the injuries and pain, Maan would be ready to participate and revive the hope of her well-wishers. Gurdev, however, found it daunting to have his mother hurt and suffer serious injuries, that too in a foreign country.

Media and Family Criticism

In one interview, an Indian journalist criticised Gurdev for pushing his centenarian mother into international competitions. Wouldn't it have been wiser and safer to keep the aged granny resting at home whiling away her twilight years in peace and quiet, he was asked. Gurdev simply refused to answer such negative questions. He believes his job is to motivate people to live an active life, a mantra he follows even today. He says that little do people understand that the thumb rule for longevity is 'freedom of movement' and helping a person to chase and achieve that is the formula for avoiding invisibility in later years. The innumerable falls during or before events instead helped build Maan's stamina and fortitude and she was able to handle negative interviews, and queries of media personnel as well as overlook unkind words and jabs from her extended family. 'Living without an ambition is like simply surviving and dying long before real death hits a person,' she believed.

Maan did not set limits for herself during her training sessions and she would often trick Gurdev and exceed the recommended goals he had set for her as her coach. She found her training sessions exciting, and despite Gurdev's refusal, she set off to attempt a long jump on a hot summer day. She had witnessed her own son participating and winning in this track and field event and she wanted to try it too! She thought she would debut in the long jump at the upcoming Asian Games in Malaysia, but Gurdev was cautious about the number of events his old mother could compete in. Without understanding that this game is based on a combination of three important factors—speed, strength and agility—Maan jumped as far as she could. This trial jump which she had undertaken at the spur of the moment literally sent shock waves up her spine and caused unbearable aches and pains at that very instant.

I was with her on the day she tried the long jump, and as mentioned, the attempt did not go down well with her and when we returned to her flat, I helped her apply oil to her back and feet to ease the pain.

Aches couldn't keep her pinned down, though. I saw, how Maan refused to lie down. She simply got up from the bed to move and walk after every half hour of rest. She did not give in to the pain and the duo, a 105-year-old and her 83-year-old son managed quite well on their own without any support of other family members. Gurdev chose to stay calm and while he did consider seeing a doctor as a last resort, he knew exactly what the doctor would do—prescribe a painkiller and on knowing Maan's age, 'doctors would end up panicking more than the patient,' he said.

The after-effects of painkillers were well-known to both and they knew that the best cure were natural remedies—a healthy diet and massage. With positivity and patience, she surmounted this hurdle, and within two days, Maan was even stitching a new pillow cover!

In conditions, where even basic normal movements were restricted by doctors for a patient with severe back injuries, Maan's determination led her to travel the whole world! She wasn't a bit worried about long flight journeys and jet lag. At her age, each passing day is considered as a bonus, an incentive from the Creator. She declined the idea of popping pills for physical stress, and opted for Indian systems of medicine—Ayurveda, Naturopathy, Unani, Yoga, Siddha, and Homeopathy—all these allowed her body to freely produce natural painkillers without being obstructed by contemporary methods of treatments. But, sometimes, falls ahead of every competition during training sessions would compel Gurdev to use the prescribed treatment by the international doctors accessible at that time. Doctors would give her medicines, yet would hesitate to recommend that she continue with the games. They were sometimes baffled by the spiritual gift she had of curing herself by a seemingly invisible Divine hand. Every time before she took a pill, she repeated the following verse from the *Satguru Sri Guru Granth Sahib Ji*:

'*Mērā Baid Gurū Gōvindā Har Har Nām Aukhadh Mukh Dēvai Kātai Jam Kī Phandhā*'[2]
—*Guru Arjan Dev, Sri Guru Granth Sahib*

'My doctor and healer is my Lord, the Lord of the Universe. He has placed the medicine of His name in my mouth and saves me from the loop of death!'

How to Build Your Resilience
1. Rising back after every fall is a trait that we all need to learn early on, like Maan learnt from her difficult childhood.
2. Do not limit yourself; set realistic goals, but, at times, try a long jump!
3. This long jump might hurt, but do not pay heed to aches.
4. Sometimes, we need to turn a deaf ear to criticism. Use your own judgement, instead.
5. Grandparents play an important role in nurturing little minds, so listen to their parables.
6. Stay calm; it will help you to make better decisions.

Chapter 14

HOLE IN A POCKET

Maan never grew up in the lap of luxury! Her truth was opposite to what the media often depicted about her life. Her husband's pension was the only source of income and while this kept the cash flowing in, it was just about enough to meet her basic needs. This was her top priority, and sometimes, she struggled even to meet her essential expenses. Furthermore, there were often inordinate delays by the government in updating her bank account. Yet, she hesitated to ask any of her children for money.

By no means did her medals and plaques or her worldwide fame and exposure guarantee them a financially secure life. There were no special provisions in the form of grants by the government to support her endeavours. Gurdev would struggle to fund their travel and other arrangements for facilitating his mother to compete at national and international levels. He also began to dip into his life's savings to support his mother's athletic pursuits. They could endure the expenses involved in participating at national level games, but the cost of flight tickets and accommodation in foreign countries began eating into his pocket. Working out the financials became a recurring task before every international tournament. 'No insurance company had the courage to offer my athlete mother an insurance coverage. We bore the expenses for all the international competitions, including the first national event in which my mother and I participated. That was till my mother became the mascot of Pinkathon,' Gurdev said.

When even her growing popularity failed to ensure their basic survival, Maan would look at her two-room flat with its tiny kitchenette in the university campus, and she would be instantly grateful. By thinking thus, she would begin focusing on the blessings she had, rather than think about the lack of things in her life. They had a tiny room with no space to place two single beds parallel to each other, so they opted for an L-shaped arrangement. Her photos in simple frames lined one wall and a series of medals hung from hooks in the same room. They managed in a miniature kitchen with a steamer and an electric plate for preparing their meals. To top it all, there was a regular midday power outage and sometimes, Gurdev could not serve Maan a cooked meal after a tedious training session. Their only alternative was to wait for the electricity or to sustain themselves on water and Kefir. Nevertheless, there was no room for grievances in Maan's life. Instead of complaining about the many inadequacies in their life, Maan would rather be in gratitude to the Divine even if she was starving!

> **Wealthy in Spirit and Body**
> They did not live grandly, and had no television, washing machine, or even a double door refrigerator in their little house. It was largely devoid of all modern appliances, but despite this, Maan was the wealthiest centenarian who possessed a physical body that was in good shape and free from ailments! How many of us can boast of possessing such good fortune?
> She advocated simple living and always declined to accept materialistic possessions as she believed these to be the root cause of the five evils troubling everybody on earth, namely *kaam* (lust), *krodh* (anger), *lobh* (greed), *moh* (strong attachment to worldly possessions and relationships) and *ahankara* (pride due to material possessions, intelligence, or power).[1]

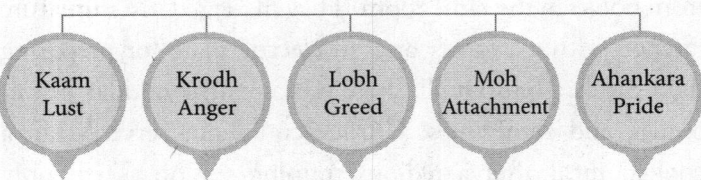

Figure 1: The Five Vices of a Human Life

Maan lived an undemanding, simple life and proclaimed, '*santokh te sabar hona chahida, je ucha jeewan jeena hai,*'— 'Contentment and patience is essential if one aims to live an exemplary life.' Seek only from Him—the one who resides in all of us!' She was a deep thinker who was cautious about what she asked for. Throughout the day, she would scan her desires by reciting the following couplet from *Jap Ji Sahib:*

> '*Mat vich ratan javāhar mānik jē ik Gur kī sikh suni*
> *Gurā ik dēh bujhāī*
> *Sabhanā jīā kā ik dātā sō mai visar n jāī*'[2]
> **—Guru Nanak, Sri Guru Granth Sahib**

Maan was blessed to recite, understand and practically live the teachings embodied in this couplet. Translated, it means: 'Within the mind are gems, jewels and rubies, if you listen to the Guru's teachings, even once. The Guru has given me this one understanding: there is only the One, the Giver of all souls. May I never forget Him.'

> **Maan's Simple Life Philosophy**
> Maan based her life on simple spiritual and strong ideologies, and understood the world's condition perfectly. She believed that outer influences or the freedom of choice given to individuals cannot, by itself assure integrity and honesty. One also needs to invoke one's own intellect, sense of morality, and self-discipline

and nurture it. She believed that education, scientific knowledge, technical skills or independence played no distinct role in enhancing self-control. She aimed to live a truthful life, one in which she would never hurt anyone's feelings. That was her simple philosophy to live a happy and content life.

Medals hanging on the wall of Maan's Punjabi University flat

Chapter 15

WHAT MADE MAAN RUN?

Maan's routine over decades had been almost the same, but she was never tired of it. She could be happy sitting in the park watching a butterfly or her eyes would follow a firefly glowing in the dark and feel a surge of joy within her heart. She had no qualms in performing the same task consistently over the years, and she applied a somewhat similar philosophy in her professional life too! She had learnt that the only way to achieve perfection and to meet a goal was by repeating the action as often as possible.

Ever since her childhood, she had been accustomed to household chores and running errands for the elders in the house. Later, her job as a nanny, mother, and a wife followed and often twenty-four hours in a day seemed insufficient to meet all her responsibilities. Maan would inevitably compromise on her sleep. It was a compulsion for her to wake up at 4 am every day. All through her childhood, she had followed this religiously and within no time, she had reached adulthood. Her circadian rhythms controlled her life processes, and most importantly, her hormones were always in her favour!

Bathing for Maan was more than just a question of maintaining personal hygiene. She was usually finished with her morning rituals before sunrise, but in the foggy winters of Punjab, she would shift her timings from 4 am to 6 am. She would regularly immerse herself in water and considered this ritual as a powerful, purifying force. It revived her body from the activities of the previous day, prepared her for her training sessions and also provided therapeutic healing.

She had no one to help her with her domestic chores and did them all on her own. This included washing clothes. She had never been a burden on anyone and did not want to indulge herself, ever. 'Pampering is a curse,' was her opinion. It led to human suffering and was a major reason for problems in one's life, both psychological and physical.

That's why Maan and Gurdev rejected appliances for assistance in cooking. They used their hands for completing all their regular household jobs. With a firm voice, Maan once told me that 'Superfluous love of an Indian mother for her son makes him dependent and he fails to develop commonsense for little things in life.'

Another daily activity was worshipping the divine and

praying. Her days began with warm gratitude for all that she had, especially a disease-free body which was her most prized possession. While Maan could survive without food whenever there were untimely power cuts (they cooked using an induction cooktop), her daily dose of *Shabad*, which literally means the Word—the doctrine of scripture, holy hymns to the divine was an absolute integral part of her daily diet.[1] *Shabad* was the mental food that she required every day. Without fail, she recited her morning prayers that included *Jap Ji Sahib, Jaap Sahib, Tav Prasad Savaiye, Chaupai Sahib* and *Anand Sahib,* and entered into deep conversation with her Creator! After prayers, Gurdev without fail, served her Kefir, a fermented probiotic drink cultured from kefir grains. She drank it daily at 7 am.

> **Maan's Training Regimen**
> Gurdev planned her training courses mostly on alternate days. During her rest days, she enjoyed casual walks in a common balcony that lined the flats where she lived. Maan's third floor accommodation took care of much-needed cardiovascular fitness for a sportsperson of her age. She gained aerobic benefits by climbing up and down the stairs. She followed no specific rules for her general warm-up exercises, but did arm circles, side shuffles, and leg swings for flexibility. She did these religiously before training commenced. After a short warm-up session, Maan began with a slow, 100-metre

run followed by a faster 100-metre run with a little rest at intervals as instructed by her coach.

During these breaks, Gurdev would pay special attention to her breath. He would stress upon proper breathing as this regulated muscle power by monitoring transfer of oxygen in the body. Appropriate breathing techniques greatly aid in relaxation of muscles, during and after training. Gurdev used this technique to improve Maan's performance and it greatly helped in reducing her timings. Preventing injuries, increasing blood flow, and improving concentration during the performance were the additional benefits that Maan received by breathing right. Most importantly, proper breathing and maintaining a correct posture during practice kept her active and in high spirits throughout the day.

Maan looked forward to achieving more and more in the athletics arena. She gradually moved from 200 metre to 400 metre races, shot put and javelin throw. At the start of her training sessions with warmup stretches and exercises, Gurdev ensured that cool down exercises were not missed.

Early morning training hours were the most valuable and productive for Maan. Students practising on the same grounds would line up by the tracks to watch her run. She was a familiar, much-loved figure for the university staff who also watched her practice and would take turns to touch her feet.

Touching an elder's feet is an integral part of Indian culture and Maan would shower blessings on them with a heart drenched in love. These short meetings with young aspiring athletes prompted Maan to keep living in the university campus. Maan usually returned to her flat after morning practice, then rested routinely for an hour from 9 am to 10 am. A couple of times in the week, she would accompany her son for grocery shopping.

On his return from the grounds, it was Gurdev's responsibility to prepare breakfast both for his mother and himself. Though they lived by themselves, the university's on campus residents never made them feel alone. Neighbours often visited Maan to take her advice on life, and every time they would go back more clear-headed and enriched by the interaction. Sometimes, working mothers would leave their children with the oldest granny in the campus. She was a multi-tasker who could swiftly stitch a salwar suit while doubling up as a babysitter at the same time. Tantrum-throwing toddlers would miraculously calm down in her presence and happily sleep on her lap while she continued to do other jobs with her hands. The little ones were assigned the task of counting rice, so this way, both remained occupied. With such an accommodating nature, Maan kept her neighbours happy. No money ever exchanged hands for these babysitting favours. Helping neighbours is an accepted social behaviour in a country like India.

During this time, Gurdev would be busy putting together ingredients for lunch—which he prepared and served to his mother at 1 pm. They took turns in serving each other. After finishing her own meal, she would gracefully, without fail, set the plate for her son. If they had unexpected visitors, they happily shared their simple meal with them. Maan was a pure *Hindustani* by heart, and believed in the adage that 'guests should never return empty-handed.' She found pleasure in sharing a portion of her life with others whether on the practice ground or at home. Maan never committed the cardinal sin of resting immediately after meals, so she would clean up and do the dishes. Then she would organise the kitchen and put things away. Only after all the chores were done would she settle down for her afternoon siesta!

Whenever she found time in between her social commitments, she would grab the opportunity to visit the Gurudwara located within the premises of the university campus. On the way, she would stop to commune with trees, her lifelong friends! Trees had been her evergreen companions and saviours. Passers-by frequently stopped to watch the old grandmother hugging trees as if in gratitude. She said that she could listen and feel the vibes of her beloved childhood buddies when she went around hugging trees. Her bonding and communion with trees was lifelong! She would say, '*Rukh mera pakka pariwar hai, jo kade saath ni chad da*'— Trees are my permanent family members and they never leave me.

Just like every morning began with the Lord's name, so also the tone for the second half of the day was set with evening prayers. Sitting next to each other, the mother-son duo would recite their prayers together. After sunset, *Rehras Sahib* uplifted their evenings while they recited the *Kirtan Sohila* before they retired to bed! Every day, from 5.30 pm to 6.30 pm, she listened to *Gurbani Katha* (explanation of the verses of the Sri Guru Granth Sahib with reference to stories and events) that played live on Khalsa FM. In between, Gurdev served her a daily dose of seasonal herbal teas. In hot weather, Gurdev would serve her tea only when it cooled down to room temperature.

Maan had no interest in social media. Gurdev was her only source who connected her to the digital world. Sometimes, she would ask Gurdev to share funny WhatsApp forwards and these tickled her pink! In the evening, students would simply step in to have a glimpse of *Biji*. Athletes would visit seeking Maan's blessings, just before leaving for national or international tournaments. Maan's hand on their heads was a mark of blessing and encouragement for these young students, and they believed she would prove to be their lucky mascot.

'*Biji de charan paeke lagda hai rabb de charan chu laye*'— 'Touching *Biji's* feet is like bowing down before the Lord,' they would say. After these visits, which cheered her up as well as it did them, she would take her last meal of the day and retire by 9 pm.

Maan's Dawn-to-Dusk Routine Prepared Her for Her Runs!

Merely adhering to a rigorous training schedule was not what prompted Maan to run. It was her century-old journey from dawn-to-dusk, and the little things that she did on a daily basis that gave her so much energy. Follow your old grandma's routine and benefit from her wisdom:

1. Water is one of the five elements that we are made up of, so a bath is essential for our body and for our soul.
2. *Nitnem*—say your daily prayers.
3. Exercise both to relax and to keep fit.
4. Inhale, exhale, repeat—but if you learn the art of HOLD in between, miracles begin to happen.
5. Share a portion of your life with others around you and do not forget to include trees and nature around you.
6. Remember, sleeping immediately after meals is a sin.
7. Ask yourself: Do small nuclear families living in tiny flats need domestic helpers?

Maan Kaur chopping, doing the dishes and hugging a tree on her way to the training ground

Chapter 16

MAAN'S SECRETS TO LONGEVITY

People often wondered how Maan apparently had the key to the elixir of youth. Was she ageing more slowly than others? Was her body abnormal? Where was she deriving all her energy from? Was she vibrating at a higher frequency? The world was desperate for answers, including me, so I probed further. She was forthcoming in her answers.

Burning with curiosity, interviewers would diligently try to unravel the mystery behind the number, 101. Media personnel had regularly shared some bits of scattered information about the life of the sprightly great-grandmother. But clever one-liners on social media rarely tell you the true story.

Maan spent several hours detailing her food choices. She would willingly share this with the world at various inaugural platforms including sports events. Her aim was to promote a healthy, and stable society. Her goal was to educate young parents about the importance of a healthy lifestyle. She felt it was they who were the most susceptible to online food services that delivered food at their doorstep on a single click! In an increasingly hectic world, where the woman of the house is also busy proving her mettle at the workplace, one can hardly expect her to cook for the family, so the food is mostly outsourced or cooked in the latest electrical appliances—microwaves or air fryers which aid in quick preparation. Thus, working mothers, try to fill emotional gaps created by their busy schedules by offering packaged and ready-to-eat tasty food to their children. They do not visualise the long-term damage that regular consumption of popular fast-foods can cause to their family's future health. Maan was totally against current food trends and opposed such a fast-paced lifestyle.

The thirteen Magic Mantras that guided her life:

> **Mantra # 1**
> Maan's first mantra to maintain fitness was maintaining a healthy work-life balance along with a well-planned diet.

Food was as important as religion to Maan! She had been a cautious eater at all stages of her life. In her youth, she had eaten her share of 'heavy' food—full of flavours, laden with *ghee* (clarified butter), but she had always been mindful of the portions on her plate. As a nanny in the Maharaja's palace, she had seen the best sweets and delicacies of the world, but she hesitated to accept these even when offered by the Ranis. She would eat only after sharing food with her children, and she would bring back home the gifts and distribute them equally among her family members. Maintaining a balanced diet was an integral part of Maan's life and she said that eating healthy had shielded her from chronic diseases. Moreover, she had been active all through and this gave her immense satisfaction.

Gurdev began his own personal research on health and diseases after his wife succumbed to high blood sugar levels when she was only sixty. He began reading books like *Back to Nature for Healthy Living; Eat to Live: The Revolutionary Formula for Fast and Sustained Weight Loss; How a Man Stays Young*, and *The Liver Cleansing Diet*. He reflected upon varied dietary plans and was intrigued by the natural healing that food provided. These books supplied detailed recipes by leading health experts to improve overall health and he planned Maan's diet, accordingly. He understood that the only source of longevity and good health in the long run was a well-planned diet. He extensively started to follow what he read, and implemented the same in their daily diet. But, despite Maan's and Gurdev's sincere efforts, they were unable to make their NRI grandchildren understand the benefits of healthy living.

Maan's recounted her US-based relative admitting that several members of his family were suffering from diabetes because of their inclination for chicken sausage and high sodium packaged meat which they ate for all three meals. Similarly, the rest of her family could not understand the fuss their athletic super-grandmother made about food. It was because of this that Maan chose to live an independent and disciplined life with her son in Patiala and often turned down invitations for visiting these relatives who lived abroad.

> **Mantra # 2**
> Own up to the responsibility of cooking your own meals.

Gurdev judiciously took upon himself, the responsibility for cooking the healthiest meals, and left no stone unturned to prepare special recipes. As a result, both Maan and he ate the best, most nutritious and healthy food. Gurdev regretted the unexpected loss of his wife at an early age, mainly due to ignorance about food habits. This made him apply his education and the acquired agricultural skills he had learned while working for Punjab Agricultural University in service of society, after he himself had retired.

Maan's passion and determination to see a world free from the pain of chronic diseases motivated her to provide consultancy services to everyone who contacted her. In a typical day, she would often allot an hour to listen to the queries of people on the phone, and would also reply to their queries on social media with Gurdev's help.

'We are what we eat,' she believed and food can either elevate our performance or can take away all the right energy and leave us feeling like a sack of potatoes, she would often say.

At Patiala, she provided guidance to university students and educated them about the significant association of the right nutrition, rest and performance on the track-field. A student's failure as an athlete, and his sufferings from prolonged weakness was cured following dietary suggestions made by Maan. Her food plan worked like medicine and in a few cases, some of the people she met on her overseas athletic meets as in Canada and Malaysia, followed her diet recommendations and they were able to stop their regular medication prescribed by doctors.

Her meals were simple and eaten at regular schedules. There was no hidden treasure in them to preserve her longevity. Every common man in India eats the same food that Maan was served, but there was a huge difference in how Gurdev prepared it. He was mindful from the first step of procuring the food till it was laid on Maan's plate. Wheat and pulses were usually gifted by his friend, Gurmail Singh, who grew them in his own agricultural land located in Nabha, 27 kilometres from Patiala. Gurdev used this wheat, which was free from processing and enzymatic polishing, to prepare their meals.

The front yard of the university's residential flats was utilised for growing seasonal produce by the employees residing in the campus. Gurdev would collect vegetables from the professors who were pleased to share their agricultural produce with the two legends. Darshan Singh, another one of Gurdev's friends who lived in Nurpur Bedi, near Anandpur Sahib in Punjab, occasionally paid them a visit carrying fresh fruits from his farmhouse. These were helpful, but they would also procure their own groceries from the local market.

> **Mantra # 3**
> Trust your instincts and choose seasonal vegetables with high water content.

For her daily needs, she applied her discerning eye to differentiate between pure, organic produce and vegetables grown with the help of chemical fertilizers. Maan relied on her instincts to choose the right variety of vegetables. She chose healthy alternatives if she suspected their purity, and strictly avoided any kind of adulterated and processed kitchen ingredients. She avoided eating tomatoes and capsicum, as it was common to spray them with pesticides and chemicals. Maan preferred to buy tomatoes during June and July, as this was the period when they are grown in the upper regions of Himachal Pradesh, and the harvested crop then finds its way into northern markets.[1] She also picked up vegetables that were easy to digest like *tori* (snake gourd), bottle gourd and pumpkin.

She refrained from eating seed-bearing vegetables, and agricultural produce with low water content as it takes longer for the body to break-down these vegetables. She was equally mindful about the milk she drank. She would trust milk only from a special booth located within the campus and would also purchase from the local vendor inside the area.

> **Mantra # 4**
> Sprouting, steam cooking, choosing the right utensils and showing the pressure cooker, the exit door of your kitchen is equally important.

Even though her meals were simple, she followed the same menu for more than two decades. Preparing this plain food in the manner in which she liked it was Gurdev's main focus. He followed a standard way of treating vegetables to ensure complete absorption of nutrients. From washing till cooking and serving, he used an alarm clock for the process! All the vegetables were steam-cooked and a pan without a lid was used for preparing porridge and *sabudana* (sago).

Their cooking utensils were also special. According to Maan, a wrong container can strip away the benefits of the cooked food, and can turn the meal into something poisonous and indigestible. The first thing she shunned was the pressure cooker. She advocated the advantages of a silent, whistle-free kitchen, and educated me on how pressure-cooking in a short time span cooks by simply exploding the food, and rupturing its vital energy or *prana,* thereby killing all nutrients available in positive pranic foods like ash gourd, whole grains, fresh seasonal vegetables, beans and lentils.

Steam cooking according to Gurdev preserves nutrients, and this slow preparation method was applied on pulses, too. The food he cooked passed through a rigid process before actually being cooked! Sprouting was another magic process that he liberally applied to his cooking style. He sprouted everything from legumes to so-called superfood seeds.

> **Benefits of sprouting**
> - Enhances nutritional value of food
> - Improves metabolism and digestion
> - Repairs capillaries
> - Helps in maintaining healthy weight
> - Improves immune system
> - Protects from cancer

Sprouting achieves all this by increasing the glucoraphanin present in cruciferous vegetables.

> **Mantra # 5**
> Believe in the magic of black gram; it isn't a feast just for horses.

Black gram or black *chana*, was her power-booster food which served as a midday meal, and also doubled up as her healthy snack throughout the day. Gurdev soaked at least five kg of the legume in water overnight, and steamed a handful before serving to his mother. This versatile gram, which is considered a feast for horses, provided sufficient amount of protein and stamina to carry out her training sessions. This 'horse gram' as it is popularly called in some parts of India aided in curbing Maan's hunger pangs during her long flight journeys, when Gurdev was unable to carry a cooked meal.

Mantra # 6
Regular wheat chapatis with a twist.

Maan followed the staple diet of Punjab and ate wheat chapati for lunch. However, it was made from a special variation in the wheat that was engineered by Gurdev. It allowed Maan to create magic in the track-fields. The benefits of this common diet were manifold.

Follow the steps that Gurdev used while preparing Maan's special wheat chapatis:

1. He would stock a sack of ten kilograms of whole wheat in their only spare room.
2. After cleaning and rinsing the required quantity of wheat for the next day's meal, he would leave it in a container with pores, overnight.
3. In the morning, using a little water, Maan would

grind the wheat with its tiny sprouts to make a batter quite different to the regular dough that is normally used for making chapatis in Indian homes.
4. Gurdev would make these chapatis by spreading this wheat batter on a hot pan.
5. Finally, he would cook it on a low flame and serve them hot.

Eating wheat in this form is a boon for curing diabetes and helps in flushing out toxins from the body, he explained. 'Its taste is appealing to the tongue, too,' Maan stated. With this specified wheat diet, they successfully treated many diabetic patients, both in India and abroad.

> **Mantra # 7**
> Sprout broccoli seeds and drink tap water but only after thorough research.

Broccoli seeds were next on Maan's sacred diet bucket list. She used a sprouter to prepare the broccoli seeds. Five tablespoons of seeds were added to a bowl and she would first thoroughly rinse out the dirt. After soaking the seeds for eight to twelve hours, she would drain off the water and the seeds were once again rinsed with cool fresh water.

The seeds were then transferred to the sprouting vessel for the next eight to ten hours, away from direct sunlight. She repeated the cleaning, soaking and transferring process till the seeds developed sprouts of about half-inch to one inch length. For four to five consecutive days, these steps were repeated. Maan would often remind her son to keep a constant vigil on it, just to spot if the tiny broccoli seeds changed colour to yellowish green, till sprouts emerged after four days. Gurdev served this nutrient-rich food to Maan every alternate day. The sulforaphane present in the broccoli sprouts prevents various neurodegenerative and cardiovascular diseases.[2] For the complete sprouting process, they used fresh water directly from the tap.

The Case Against Reverse Osmosis
The RO (reverse osmosis) filter installed by the university staff in her kitchen hung on the wall, still in its sealed plastic cover. Maan had a deep understanding of the RO process and claimed that it must be avoided wherever possible. Blind belief is dangerous so she preferred that Gurdev conducted detailed research before the two tried out something new in their daily regimen. They got their water tested and further analysis of the physicochemical parameters of the university tap water verified its safety. She also confirmed about its chemical properties of hardness, dissolved salts, chloride and fluoride to ensure that it was safe for drinking. Moreover, tap water has the necessary minerals needed for the body which is entirely lost in the process of reverse osmosis.

Mantra # 8
We need refrigerators, not wardrobes!

The next indispensable appliance without which a kitchen in the twenty-first century would lose its identity, the refrigerator, was also kept in their spare room. They owned an antique compartment-type refrigerator and used it to store raw, uncooked food items which are available only during a specific season of the year like drumsticks. These were stored for Maan's regular consumption.

A look at her refrigerator would indicate immediately how the rest of us have thrown our bodies off kilter. It was more of a laboratory unlike usual modern refrigerators. Now, refrigerators, are like wardrobe cabinets which can be used to store at least a week's supply of cooked food. There is a belief that the larger the size of your refrigerator, the larger the magnitude of the diseases that afflicts the family! 'It covers half of the kitchen area, and the bigger the size of the fridge, the harder it will be to correct the health of the people in the family,' Maan said to me.

Their guestroom resembled a mini nursery, and also doubled up as Gurdev's research lab-cum-storeroom—where he grew wheat grass, lemon grass, and stored freshly gifted sacks of wheat. This room was also used to pile up the ingredients for their evening tea. Besides these fresh leaves, dry fruits like almonds, walnuts and dates, nature's little power-packed snacks were also taken regularly for their rich protein, mineral, and vitamin content. Maan's diet also included chia seeds for their high amounts of omega-3 fatty acids, calcium, protein, and phosphorus.

> **Mantra # 9**
> Making Kefir, Maan's key food.

Maan substituted milk and curd with Kefir. She considered this probiotic drink perfect for a healthy gut. This cultured super-food is made using milk, water or coconut with kefir grains. She would wake up and drink a glass of kefir on an empty stomach, every morning. It provided her with the right energy before her training sessions. Recent literature based on scientific research has confirmed the innumerable benefits of this versatile drink. Listed here are the results of drinking a glass of milk kefir:[3,4]

1. Improves the immune system by providing essential minerals, proteins, vitamins and calcium to the body.
2. Relaxes the nervous system.
3. Reduces the side-effects of antibiotics and works as a natural antibiotic by eliminating harmful bacteria from body.
4. Benefits those who are lactose intolerant.
5. Treats blood sugar imbalances, diarrhoea, urinary tract infections, and allergies.
6. Regulates blood pressure.
7. Aids in cancer prevention.

8. Benefits patients suffering from AIDS, tumours, and herpes.
9. Positively impacts people facing chronic fatigue syndrome.

Maan was on a mission to distribute kefir grains nation-wide as it was this one ingredient that safeguarded her from so many diseases common among older adults. From Bombay and Pune in the west; Amritsar, Patiala, Chandigarh, Ludhiana, Jalandhar, and Shimla in the north; Bangalore, and Hyderabad in the south and Kolkata, Kumardhubi in the east, she propagated these magical grains during her tours. Kefir also works exceptionally well on people suffering from depression, and anxiety by improving the connection between the brain and the gut. And here's the plus-point: you don't need cooking gas, or need to chop and saute while preparing milk kefir. The only ingredient that you need besides kefir grains, is pasteurised milk—cow, buffalo, goat, coconut, or almond.

Making a Probiotic Drink with Kefir Grains

Step 1: Place one tablespoon of kefir grains in a glass jar or non-metal bowl.

Step 2: Add four cups of milk set at room temperature or pour the pasteurised milk which you receive from your vendor directly into the bowl and cover it with a breathable cloth.

Step 3: Set it aside for fermentation at room temperature for 18-24 hours. In winters, it takes longer for the grains to ferment the milk, so wait until the milk turns thick like curd and smells fermented.
Step 4: Strain the kefir through a non-metallic sieve.
Step 5: Start a new batch with the grains left behind in the sieve, or store the grains in the refrigerator until you consume the first batch of kefir.

> **Mantra # 10**
> Eat in moderation and in a meditative mood. Treat food as sacred and divine, like our morning prayers.

Gobbling up food just for taste was something Maan never quite understood. *Paisa kamande roti vaste, hor roti vi baeke nai khadi te jiwan kaeda swarange,* she would often say. Translated, this means, 'We earn to fill our stomach, but if we cannot eat food in a peaceful state, then how can we improve our lives?' The message was that we must take care of our basics, and the rest will take care of itself.

> **Mantra # 11**
> Massage—a therapy that Maan learnt from her own granny!

Maan advocated massage as the simplest and the cheapest way to decrease muscular tension after training sessions. She also suggested swapping moisturisers for aloe vera. In summers, she would apply home grown aloe vera, twice or thrice weekly to relieve stress and heat from her body. During winters, she used mustard oil to massage her skin. She remembered her granny narrating the benefits of a mustard oil massage to her, approximately a hundred years earlier.

> **Mantra # 12**
> Herbal teas and juices as functional foods.

Maan was very particular about evening tea which she would sip together with her son while listening to the *Gurbani katha*. For their evening tea, they used raw, dried herbal leaves or the following:
- Ripened drumstick seeds
- *Mulethi* (licorice)
- *Neem* sticks
- Eucalyptus leaves
- Amaltas flowers and leaves
- *Bael* fruit (stone apple)
- Unripe papaya
- Pomegranate peels
- *Shahtoot* (mulberry)

Tea of dried Amaltas leaves were high on the list of their priorities as it helped in maintaining good health by keeping cough, fever and stomach ailments at bay. The Amaltas flower was noted for benefits such as strengthening the heart. Gurdev considered this herbal tea essential for Maan. Unripe papaya tea was one of the healthiest drinks that Maan had; however, the bigger challenge was to find the raw form of this fruit in Punjab, as what was available in the market was usually the fully matured papaya. Accordingly, she substituted raw papaya with pomegranates, when these were in season. She used the sour yellow portion of the pomegranate fruit, just beneath the red skin, for making her evening drink. Gurdev added that this therapeutic tea was excellent for a cough and a sore throat. It also benefitted her bone health and shielded her from gut-related infections and diseases. *Shahtoot* (mulberry) tea was prepared by using dried tree leaves, as it an excellent source of calcium, iron, minerals, and antioxidants. This tea also regulates proper functioning of blood vessels.[5] *Shahtoot* is a medicinal herb used for naturally curing bad cholesterol, diabetes and heart disease.

The fruit of the moringa tree, drumsticks and its leaves and flowers were also dried, and she used the ripened drumstick seeds and its green outer skin to make tea, which acted as a filter for the arteries, regulated sugar levels, improved the immune system and more importantly, granted strength to the bones which was so important for Maan.[6]

Wheatgrass Shots

Apart from these herbal drinks, she successfully treated her age-related sleep disorders and controlled nocturia, with juices. Waking up during the nights to urinate led to mood swings and irritability which affected her performance negatively. Gurdev would himself extract wheatgrass juice from the freshly cut first leaves of the wheat, plucked from the pot placed in their living room. The duo claimed that this concoction corrected sleep patterns! If she lost vital minerals due to her overactive bladder, she regained them with these shots of wheatgrass juice. Other benefits of wheatgrass included rebuilding of damaged tissues, treating of liver and kidney-related issues, strengthening bones, improving oxygen levels and detoxifying the body.[7]

From the onset of winter, till March, red carrots would flood the market, and Maan diligently extracted the juice of this seasonal vegetable. She was unsuccessful in getting the Patiala *mandi* (vegetable market) vendors to procure regular supplies of parsley and celery, so she made it mandatory to nourish herself with the juice of parsley, celery and beetroot during her international travels to Canada, Malaysia, New Zealand and other countries.

> **Mantra # 13**
> Trust and unlock the secrets of traditional medicines.

Maan avoided allopathy medicines because she knew that such remedies only meant a fast but temporary cure. Her belief was that strong drugs ultimately degraded the overall system. 'Painkillers and antibiotics treat you brutally,' Maan would reiterate, and would resist seeing a doctor. Her home-based herbal treatments worked well and guaranteed an evergreen, active life irrespective of routine cyclic, environmental and seasonal changes.

What Maan Ate for Breakfast, Lunch, and Dinner
Maan religiously kept following the dietary guidelines laid down by her son. She was strict with herself and never indulged her taste buds. 'We are slaves to our senses and once caught, it is difficult to come out of its deadly trap,' she would say. For breakfast, her staple was *sabudana* (sago) mixed with jaggery, or sprouted wheat chapati with some herbs and salt added to the wheat batter. Seasonal vegetables in summers, and *sarson* (mustard), *methi* (fenugreek leaves) or spinach in winters with sprouted wheat chapati were standard for lunch. Dinners were mainly of oatmeal mixed with lentils or *khichdi*.

Listen to Your Body and to the Seasons
Maan was in sync with her body clock, and paid attention to her daily rhythm. People of her era needed no education on the type of food that should be eaten. They believed in following their natural instincts and eating seasonal

food, unlike the present generation where media and slick advertising decides on what must appear on our tables. What our present media terms as 'superfoods' was being regularly eaten by her generation.

Maan believed that 'Everything is inside us, so listen to your inner voice and you'll become superhuman.' Basic ingredients of Indian cuisine like garlic, ginger, and turmeric now being labelled as superfoods was staple fare to people of her generation. Food grown a century ago was naturally organic, grown without artificial chemical fertilizers unlike the fancy 'organic' label it now sells under at double the price. Maan may have had no official degree, but she had access to age-old wisdom and when she would see what the world had come to in this progressive, mechanised age, it was hard for her not to grow disheartened.

Gurdev cooking

Drumstick seeds for evening tea

Chapter 17

MAAN, A VALUED CELEBRITY!

A decade ago, Maan's life had suddenly taken an incredible turn and she began to be hailed as an inspiration to humankind. Age could not match up to her energy levels that was so visible in the spark in her eyes! Despite her large, old-fashioned spectacles, one could easily discern the twinkle in her eyes.

Maan had unexpectedly become a media personality and all of a sudden, you could watch her on national news, in TV programmes and on YouTube. But this did not go to her head and she consciously refrained from basking in the admiration and glamour with which the world suddenly began to see her. Yet, sometimes she nourished her spirit and basked in the glory of the first compliment received from the president of the National Masters Athletics Championships held in Chandigarh who referred to Maan as *'Sada Gold Medal Hai'*—Maan is our gold medal. The president's compliment was the reason Maan kickstarted her shining career in the international arena.

Soon after fame kissed her brow, Gurdev felt the need for a makeover in his mother's appearance. The old spectacles were replaced by a colourful, trendy purple frame. However, the glamour did not allow her to discard the five *Kakars* of Sikhism that she adored and continued to wear even at the world championships.

The five symbols that she wore on her person denote cohesion and cooperation among the community at large. She could vaguely recall the sacred Sikh initiation ceremony, *Amrit Sanchar,* when she was introduced to *Khande di Pahul* or *Amrit* during her childhood. Since then, she had worn the five K's namely, *Kesh* (unshorn hair as a symbol of respect towards the Creator's wisdom in creating the human form; scientifically, hair preserves mental stability being an element of ether), *Kangha* (comb tucked into her hair), *Kara* (circular stainless steel or iron bangle), *Kachera* (prescribed shorts), and *Kirpan* (sword suspended from a belt across the chest).[1] She followed this code of conduct wherever she went, including at international games. This defined her commitment, sense of morality, self-discipline and attitude towards life!

She had not for one moment deviated from the 'Sikh code of discipline; *Rehat Maryada,* and the Sikh symbols which originated in the eighteenth century when the Sikh tradition was formally established by a proclamation by Sri Guru Gobind Singh (the tenth Sikh Guru) on Vaisakhi day in 1699, barely 325 years ago.[2] *Rehat* implies a way of life, thereby illustrating how a true seeker (Sikh literally means 'to learn') must live, and *Maryada* involves tradition and practice of the faith. Whenever she was being interviewed in front of the camera, Maan was always found with her head covered with a dupatta, along with her signature, heart-melting broad smile!

Smiling for the paparazzi came naturally to her, but her toothy smile necessitated the need for a set of dentures. And so, at 105, she could confidently offer her celebrity smile with rows of glinting white, removable teeth. Maan continued to spread positivity wherever she went and she would begin her interviews with a Punjabi scriptural couplet whether in Auckland, Sacramento, Toronto or India. She always addressed her fans with a spirited,

Jo Bole So Nihal
Sat Sri Akal
(Blessed is the one, who says God is a timeless truth)

Stardom did not happen overnight. It was Maan's determination that helped her take all challenges in her stride with the continuous aim of improving her own records; this attitude eventually took her from strength to strength. She became the world's fastest granny by winning a gold medal in the 100-metre sprint with a timing of 1 minute and 21 seconds at the Americas Masters Games in Vancouver. Later, Maan broke the world record of 1 minute 17 seconds, and also broke her own record by improving her performance by 7 seconds at the World Masters Games in Auckland by clocking 1:14:56 minutes! She concluded the 100-metre sprint in 1:1:87 minutes and 200 metres in 2:29:90 minutes at the World Masters Athletics championships at Sacramento. This motivated Maan to work harder and with single-minded devotion, she aimed to break her own records in all the upcoming games. New Zealand played the perfect host at the next venue after the Auckland games. And, of course, it was in New Zealand that Maan became an instant media figure.

The celebrity label brought recognition on a scale unparalleled by any previous centenarian and soon Maan was seen in headlines across the world inaugurating events and appearing as a Chief Guest on special occasions. Her lack of formal education did not hold her back from delivering speeches at these events. She could stun a huge hall with her wisdom, quick wit and her smile!

Several State universities and schools started inviting Maan for imparting life enhancing skills to their students. Panjab University, Desh Bhagat University, Chandigarh University, Punjabi University, and Khalsa College were a few of the institutions where she was invited to lecture.

Addressing members of the House of Commons of Canada taught her the appropriate way to use formal and honorific titles. In Patiala, she delivered a discourse to an elite gathering of top income tax officials from northern India. As a brand ambassador of Pinkathon, she frequently inspired women from different walks of life, and gave impromptu speeches around the country. The prestigious Akal Academy in Baru Sahib, Himachal Pradesh, invited her to stay at their campus for several months to guide residential sportspersons. She was also invited by the Delhi-based Super Sikh Foundation, where Maan flagged off the ONE RACE Half Marathon in 2017.

In the same year, she was nominated along with five other international athletes for the Laureus World Sports Awards in a new category, 'Best Sporting Moment of the Year'. She went on to inaugurate half marathons, worldwide, ranging from the '5 kilometres Run' during the Vaisakhi celebrations in New York, and also in Delhi, Bangalore, Kolkata, Chandigarh, and Patiala. Maan would turn up in rural areas of Punjab, where she was routinely asked to motivate village women. She would humbly reach the venue, long before time. In this manner, she proved motivating to so many people of all ages and races!

Maan began to be invited by top TV anchors for discussions by eminent journalists. She appeared as a guest in a Global Townhall hosted by Barkha Dutt, 'We The Women' in 2018. There were discussions on her age, sports career, health and diet. A news show DNA (Daily News and Analysis) hosted by Sudhir Chaudhary (former editor-in-chief of Zee News) also had her as their celebrity speaker and highlighted her remarkable feats and the secrets of her longevity. She was also interviewed worldwide by famed global journalists. 'This is Me,' a special show portraying Maan's life in detail was covered by the New Zealand media.

Maan could make the President jog and the Prime Minister pay heed to her advice

The world, including India's three-time PM, Narendra Modi affirmed the benefits of adopting an active lifestyle prescribed by Maan. Her efforts were recognised by top government employees and she became the face of the 'Fit India Movement,' launched on 29 August, 2019, by the Indian government with a vision to integrate fitness into the daily lives of citizens. The movement aims to bring about behavioural changes through initiatives and events in schools, colleges, universities, and villages. Maan emphasised the need for regular exercise and said that a nation could progress only if its citizens were healthy.

The whole country was awestruck by her charisma! Maan was not familiar with Bollywood stars, but even they would line up to have their photographs clicked with the superstar granny. She treated these superstars like her daughters and sons and would behave the same way—with school girls, celebrities or even with the Indian PM. Reaching out to groups with a message of equality and spreading love was her life's goal! 'We all have come from the same source, and no one is more, or less!' she would say.

> **Three Universal Blessings of Maan!**
> Whether at her humble home or at a formal event, Maan would greet everyone with the same passion and energy. Her speeches were instinctive as the language of love is universal, and her divine blessings were for the entire society. She would bestow blessings of *'Waheguru Tandrusti Bakshan'* (may the beautiful Lord bless you with a fit body) on everyone and would proclaim, *'Chardikala Vich Raho'* (always live in joy with a positive mindset) and would tell everyone, *'Rabb Naam di Daat Bakshan'* (may you always remember the Lord's name).

Maan believed that whatever she had achieved at her age was due to the Lord's benevolence. 'Only the Lord makes me win; I have no power in my frame to reach so far,' she had said while addressing the media in Auckland. She savoured attention from her international fans and on receiving applause and unconditional love on the track-field, would often break out in an impromptu *gidda* (a Punjabi folk dance). She was oblivious of the scale of her achievements, and has even been compared to the legendary 113-year-old marathon runner, Fauja Singh. *Weekender* compared her to Usain Bolt. She remained stoic!

These endorsements drew the world's attention

towards her achievements, and soon, she had become a new-age internet sensation. The Ministry of Women and Child Development conferred the Nari Shakti Puraskar in 2019 on Maan for her contribution to women empowerment. News about the 'Miracle Mom from Chandigarh' being nationally recognised spread rapidly and her family celebrated her rare feats. Erstwhile President Ram Nath Kovind presented her with the country's highest civilian honour for women. Maan was delighted to receive an invitation letter from the Union ministry that read:

'It is a matter of great pleasure to inform you that you have been selected for the prestigious Nari Shakti Puraskar, 2019, for your exceptional contribution towards women empowerment. The award carries an honorarium of Rs 2 lakh and a certificate.'[3]

Maan Kaur with her family after receiving Nari Shakti Puraskar

Chapter 18

ROOM NUMBER ONE

The Baradari Palace and Garden were built by Maharaja Rajinder Singh, Maharaja Bhupinder Singh's father, who ruled Patiala from 1876-1900. Patiala, as everyone is aware of is a leading Indian state for sports and has contributed many sportspersons to the country.

Baradari Palace, is one of the more modest palaces that dot the city of Patiala. Baradari or the twelve-door pavilion is a white, colonnade building designed by the younger brother of the Maharaja, Kaur Sahib Ranbir Singh in 1876 and is designed on the Sikh-Mughal style of architecture.[1]

The scholarly works of Professor Sahib Singh together with the records of the Patiala and East Punjab States Union (PEPSU) an erstwhile state of India that united eight princely states between 1948 and 1956 are housed in the Baradari Palace.[2] The palace has since been renovated and is currently a Heritage Hotel, Neemrana, in the Baradari Gardens. Today, this nineteenth century palace uniting the Hindustani, Mughal, and colonial style of architecture in the heart of the royal city of Punjab boasts of air-conditioned rooms with televisions, private restrooms with showers, and wooden furnishings with ancient carvings of the Maharaja's times. To keep pace with the demands of the present times and guests, the palace hotel has installed CCTV cameras, and is equipped with a wireless network and internet services.

Maan had fond memories of the palace! As a nanny serving the Maharanis, she always thought about the incredible life of the queens. While completing her daily chores at the palace, she would sometimes raise questions about the what, why, and how of her life to the Creator. 'We all have come from one source and that is You! It is Your play that some are made queens, and some like me are made to serve them.' Like any other girl, Maan always wished to be treated like a queen, and imagined that one day she, too, would sit in a *palanquin*—an enclosed litter mounted on four poles carried by four bearers on their shoulders. Maan thought of those good old days when she saw the queens in all their pomp and glory as the 'grand royal days.' In her many daydreams, she, too pictured herself as being part of royalty and was not among those who bowed down till the cavalcade passed.

She would thus fill the gaps between the real world

and her utopian vision of life. Her other coworkers had to pinch Maan to bring her back from her fanciful wanderings. In 2016, again, she asked the hotel assistant to pinch her when she was accommodated in Room Number One of the palace hotel. It was the same room where the Maharani had spent so many years! She paid attention to every little object in the room, as she relived her early life in that moment. It was like a grand homecoming! She made a detailed note of the incident and absorbed this new experience. She was reliving her role reversal after more than eighty years!

That night, she lay on the bed in the room that once belonged to the Maharani, the same Maharani that she had once served. Initially, it was difficult for her to lie down quietly as she could not believe her luck. She feared her colleagues of all those years ago would peep into the room, and Maan would wake up at the slightest noise coming from outside the window. She dreamt of the Maharaja crossing the corridor and being punished for sleeping in Room Number One!

Maan had a treasure trove of stories to tell me! She reminisced about how she once ran towards an area where commoners were not allowed entry. Those were different times, Maan said. It was easier to get the work done from someone rather than introduce a new rule into the system. Nobody dared to raise questions. Attaching the fear factor to a new rule was a foolproof trick that always worked.

But, with Maan it was not easy as she would secretly cross-check the orders, before accepting them.

She narrated another story of those times. They had been instructed not to visit certain spots around the palace because it was associated with ghost stories. Many claimed that they had heard strange, haunting music playing in these zones, especially during night hours. But it was difficult to make Maan believe these tales because of her questioning mind. Moreover, she herself was a creative story teller.

Maan and the Ghosts

One evening, she decided to venture forth on a forbidden track. When she had walked about half a mile, she saw jewels shimmering in the twilight. She ran back shouting, *'Bhoot, bhoot*—Ghost, ghost.' Maan gasped, and collected her breath after being assured by her senior colleagues that what she had seen were certainly not ghosts. She now thought she would be executed for referring to the Maharaja's entourage and his Ranis, courtesans and *darbaris* (courtiers) as ghosts! This incident made her understand that those areas were secret spots meant only for the king, and his queens and for other strange men. The sound she had heard was of the music band that accompanied the Maharaja.

'The universe pays attention to our every desire,' observed Maan. But, clarified that modern inventions of a new era are always given due consideration. 'Today, I do not wish people to bow down or clear the route that I traverse, but I try to earn their respect and love with honest labour.'

The questions raised by Maan almost eighty years ago, had been answered in the current century. She realised that conversations with the Supreme were never one-way; the Supreme Being maybe at the receiving end, when she was talking, but he had been 'listening,' she said. 'Life is full of surprises, so do not take even mundane matters for granted,' she told me.

Chapter 19

PINKATHON

Maan's celebrity status soon brought offers of branding and endorsements and these played a complementary role to her sports career. She relished life's pleasant offerings by simply seizing the day. The World Masters Games, Auckland, where Maan's magic was first noticed and recognised by the globe, was noticed by no less than actor, supermodel, entrepreneur and founder of Pinkathon, Milind Soman. He had discovered his lucky charm! With all her achievements, popularity and transcendental vision, Maan was in great demand for endorsing big brands. And so it was that she launched her career as a brand ambassador of Pinkathon.

Creating running space exclusively for women was what Pinkathon had intended at its inaugural race in December 2012. In a little more than a decade, every big Indian city is now familiar with its vision of promoting women's health and spreading awareness about breast cancer through its marathons that have women participating in 3, 5, 10-kilometre marathons and half marathons. Women—who came forward to just have a selfie clicked with the actor got impressed by the fitness targets and began participating in the run. Pinkathon, together with Maan brought a revolutionary change among Indian women by motivating them to adopt a fitter lifestyle.

As a fitness promoter, herself, she completely resonated with the primary goal of this organisation and she got her mojo working for Pinkathon, currently the biggest running platform for Indian women. She communicated her message through the Pinkathon platform—that women must include regular exercise to their daily routine. It also aided her in accomplishing her own fitness goal.

Soon, she was invited by Pinkathon's Delhi-based team for an ice-breaking session. Maan needed no further guidance! Her exposure to the international arena had always kept her abreast of changing trends in nutrition and fitness and she could answer all kinds of questions with ease. Her enthusiasm multiplied whenever she received an active audience response. Watching Maan strut about confidently on stage, the audience sang, danced, and tried matching her *gidda* beat steps. She took upon the role of a celebrity endorser and looked forward to giving her best to the event.

Her new designation demanded a lot of travel. Gurdev was equally wonderstruck at witnessing his mother's fervour combined with her enthusiasm as a committed athlete. By this time, Maan had lost count of the number of air and road journeys she had undertaken. The eagerness to meet and interact with people was her driving force. At one of the Pinkathon platforms, she described the body as a machine run by our minds. No matter what your age is, one's actions are directly dependent on how you programme your brain, she told her audience. She religiously followed her own theory.

She marched on the itinerary set by the Pinkathon team. She made innumerable public appearances and met Pinkathon fans at her own residence in Patiala, too. Apart from the four metropolitan cities, Delhi, Mumbai, Chennai, and Kolkata, Maan inaugurated marathons in prominent tier two cities, such as Pune, Hyderabad, Ahmedabad, and Bengaluru. She went as far as Guwahati in the east. Maan would improvise and deliver motivational speeches to a crowd, ten thousand-strong, taking it in her stride.

In March 2020, Pinkathon celebrated Maan's 104th birthday in Ahmedabad, and wished her success with a huge cake cutting ceremony with Milind Soman by her side. Maan again swayed the audience by moving her body and feet to the music. Whether it was at the track-field or at an award ceremony, the public started associating dancing as an integral part of Maan's persona. Maan always kept track of forthcoming Pinkathon events and continued to appear in all of them—till her last breath!

On Maan's 105th birthday, Milind Soman surprised the veteran athlete by visiting her house in Patiala. The fitness enthusiast also had a practice session at the university's track-field with Maan. This extraordinary gesture made his Pinkathon mascot unaccountably happy. Within hours, social media came abuzz with warm wishes, likes, and comments!

Chapter 20

IMMORTAL MESSAGES FOR THE MORTALS

Maan was not born into privilege, but she carved out a glittering career as an international athlete and became a leading centenarian who passed her jewels onto modern society. Here is Maan's wisdom, collected over a century and presented in a nutshell:

Consciously allocate time to three key areas for a content existence:

Work **Health** **Spiritual Practice**

According to Maan, neglecting any one of these would make one ill. She advocated maintaining a balance to avoid feelings of incompleteness and regret later in life!

Once, during a tournament, Maan stayed with a Indian-Canadian family and noticed meat at all three meals. She couldn't stop herself from saying, '*Kade hara vi kha laya karo.*'— 'Sometimes, surely, you all can eat some greens?' Maan was stunned by the response when she was told: '*Asi bakri nai jo hara khaiye.*'— 'Are we goats that we should eat greens? Years later, when Maan met the family again, she saw a change in their whole menu. The reason for this dietary change was a doctor's prescription. They had all been suffering from chronic lifestyle diseases like hypertension, diabetes, and obesity, and they regretted ignoring her sage advice.

Time is the biggest teacher, and shortly, thereafter, Maan became their diet consultant. The family approached her for guidance and she prepared a customised diet chart for them.

Every cell in our body is defined by the foods we eat, so Maan had been careful about her diet both, mental and physical! Her mindset and the environment in which she ate was another significant factor. Noise or other distractions while eating would upset her. She and Gurdev did not talk or share worldly concerns while they were eating and nourishing their bodies. The place from where the groceries were purchased and the hands used for preparing the meals were also a matter of concern for Maan. For this reason, she turned down any kind of domestic help and shared the household chores with her son, including mopping and cleaning the house. She believed that the emotion with which a cook prepared a meal is also transferred to the one who is eating; an angry or a happy cook will either pass on his anger or love to the people eating the food, she would say.

Maan discouraged the practice of eating in a restaurant or from street vendors, and her heart broke once when she saw a mother feeding an aerated drink to her seven-month-old baby. In her lectures, Maan would try to educate young mothers telling them that it was in their hands to make or break the future of their country. 'With your hard-earned money, you buy diseases in exchange. Instead, take out time to nourish yourself, eat a simple diet, and work hard to give practical shape to your goals—there are no shortcuts in life,' she would tell her audience.

'Exercise in the morning and stay away from bed during the daytime,' was another one of her signature statements.

She proved to the world that through self-discipline, a prerequisite for growth, one could achieve super human results. She would also say that 'Human beings without *sadhana* (a devotional practice or religious training leading to self-realisation) are very close to the animal kingdom.' Maan would tell them about her own personal approach towards serving her parents and elders and how that had helped her by keeping her detached from worldly affairs! Thus, she desired that children should serve their parents and advocated *seva* (selfless service). All these had played a crucial role in her childhood, and was an inseparable part of her life. Even at 105, she considered contributing towards the growth of society as her responsibility—whether it was in New Zealand's Gurudwara Sahib or at an international tournament.

Merely reading the Holy Scriptures with no attempt to implement the teachings in our daily lives, will only lead to frustration. This was her message to the world. Maan believed in action and as soon as she put on her running shoes, she would move out of the house, meet people, serve the needy, and meet the Lord as well.

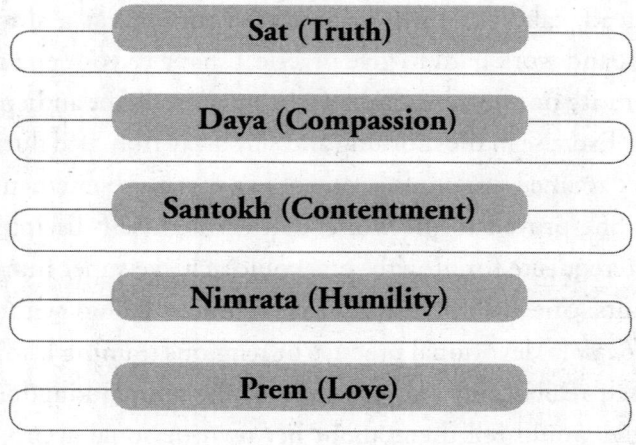

Figure 2: The Five Virtues of a Human Life

'Kade mada na bolo.'

'Avoid harsh words and watch what you say.' Maan's life demonstrated that no matter how insensitive the world or your early life experiences were, you should not let your soul stoop to low levels. A constant check on her mind through meditation, and conscious living had been her biggest teachers. She advocated that everyone should do *seva*.

Seva—Why and How?
What is seva?
Seva is a selfless and voluntary service done without any personal desires or gains. It is a doorway to liberation if done with utmost love, sincerity, humility, and by consciously keeping one's ego, aside. Seva can be social, physical, and spiritual for the welfare of society with no discrimination on the basis of caste, creed, and colour.

Why you should do seva
Seva nurtures love for the Creator and gives a feeling of fulfilment, peace and unity when you contribute towards the development and upliftment of the community.

How to do seva
Seva can be done through any of the three ways listed below:
1. *Tan* (body): Contributing in the community kitchen, polishing shoes in the temples, keeping your

> environment clean are a few ways of physical form of seva.
> 2. *Man* (mind): You can help, contributing with your mental skills such as through mentoring, or providing psychological support.
> 3. *Dhan* (material wealth): Donate one-tenth of your income earned through honest means to charities or serve the destitutes and less privileged ones.

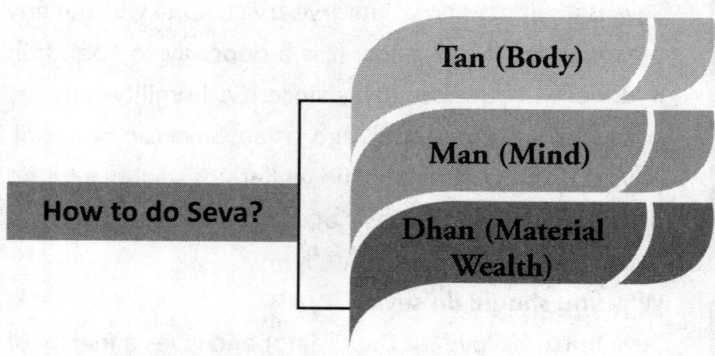

Figure 3: Types of Seva

Chapter 21

THE LAST RUN

Maan felt a sudden and intense pain in the upper right quadrant of her ribs. It indicated a problem with an organ in that area—pancreas, gallbladder, liver, right kidney, or intestines. Doctors in Patiala diagnosed her with gallbladder stones. She would need several days of rest, and would need to be careful with her movements. The thought of a surgery can create anxiety and scare patients, yet Maan's willpower helped her overcome the intensity of her pain with her cheerful demeanour. The doctors were surprised with her forbearance.

Gurdev immediately got her hospitalised and treatment began. Doctors abstained from any form of invasive surgery, and thus at 104, she was healed from the pain of her gallstones. This experience in no way shook Maan's resolve to participate in upcoming events. She concentrated on regaining her health. Her feet were aching to feel the vibration of the ground and she went to Sarawak for the Asian Games in the same year, a few months after her treatment.

Health issues and finances are the two most important factors governing the life of most people, but not for Maan. Her passion for sports ensured that Maan was not yet ready to hang her shoes, even though she had never received any sponsorship throughout her career. Pinkathon came only in her later years and was finally able to cover her travel expenses for international competitions. This provided some much-needed financial assistance.

As a sports star, Maan had been invited for inaugurations, marathon grand openings and even walking the ramp. At the Amazon India Fashion Week, Maan walked the ramp with Milind Soman. She found it no different from walking on the track-field and would have kept on walking if the actor had not prevented her from crossing the edge. After her dazzling walk, Maan was guided to join the backstage artists, but she refused and communicated with the spectators in her own language of dance, almost like Shiva communicating the meaning of the Vedas through his *tandava nritya!* Maan was like a free-flowing river. She had crossed various twists and turns and was still not tired of spreading happiness. She was unique and this attracted a large and devoted audience worldwide.

From a difficult childhood to a ceremonial existence in a palace, Maan's life had come full circle. The pomp and pageantry she had experienced with the Ranis helped prepare her for the adulation she experienced in the later years of her life. She had derived important life lessons from the complex and huge community she had served. The warmth and grace that she had learnt in her first job became an integral part of her character and this resurfaced in her public appearances in her extraordinary life as an athlete.

> **Maan: 'Human Life is a Gift'**
> Maan led a blessed life, sought after by a steady stream of visitors whom she treated with whatever limited resources she had. Some visited her as fans, others to satisfy their curiosity and some to seek her blessings. Some wanted to unlock the secrets of her longevity, while others came seeking cures for various ailments. By simply following her guidance and simple lifestyle, many could live a healthier life. Her actionable examples to improve one's lifestyle worked like a magic bullet to cure chronic diseases.

Maan once said, 'This human life is a gift and an opportunity to use this body frame for supporting society, so work towards spreading happiness around you.'

She was a trend-setter for those who were dismayed about their impending retirement. And she certainly broke all notions of traditional retirement age norms. Maan launched her career three decades after an ordinary man prepares to leave work permanently. And once in it, not once did she think of quitting. She had no plans to retire.

After receiving the Nari Shakti Puraskar, she met several of her fans who were waiting to honour her at Punjabi University. But she could interact with the staff and fellow athletes only through video chats due to the lockdown. Sitting idle was mentally tough for Maan as she had never halted in her entire life. The lockdown upset her tempo, and Covid-19 took a toll on her. Overnight, students and staff of Punjabi University abandoned the whole campus, and Maan missed meeting young athletes. She had always been surrounded by visitors and children and meeting them was like a tonic for her. More than Covid, what haunted Gurdev was the fear of his mother being attacked by her deadly childhood disease of 'loneliness.' To combat her mental fatigue, Maan's self-developed strategies rescued her again. She passed her time by watching old YouTube videos of winning medals, and of watching her fans meet her at events.

During this unprecedented phase, older people had proved to be most vulnerable as their chances of survival were the lowest.[1] Gurdev's only approach to maintain his mother's fitness levels and to keep her motivated was to keep her engaged at the track-field of Punjabi University. Throughout the pandemic, Maan focused on her training and did not skip her practice even for a single day. When the ground was closed for safety reasons, the corridor of her apartment block became her practice ground. She made sure to remain active.

The lockdown at a global level led to the postponement or cancellation of all sporting events. She had been preparing for the World Masters Games and manifested symptoms of depression when informed about the cancellation of the World Masters Athletics Canada, 2020. State events of Pinkathon and National Sports Meet were also called off. Nevertheless, she regained her lost spirits when she was invited as a chief guest at a Marathon Run in March 2021 at Kolkata.

However, the joy and sense of freedom that the invitation brought was short-lived. Weeks later, on 15 February, 2021, she experienced a stabbing pain in her abdomen. Gurdev rushed her to the famous Rajindra Hospital in Patiala. His world came to a sudden halt when doctors showed him his mother's ultrasound reports. Maan had been diagnosed with advanced levels of liver and gallbladder cancers.

For detailed investigation, Gurdev took her to PGI, Chandigarh, where her diagnosis was confirmed by the post graduate institute. But he had no time to exhibit his grief. This news could torpedo Maan's dream of running in the Olympics in Japan, and he could not muster the courage to reveal this to his mother.

Gurdev was eighty-two himself, but nevertheless, he

travelled extensively to various parts of the country for her treatment. He took Maan to Indore and consulted specialists. Doctors denied oncological treatments such as chemotherapy and radiotherapy to Maan, due to her age. Though she was not suffering from any other chronic disease and was not taking any medication, her age came in the way and barred her from receiving treatment.

> **'Miracle diet to cure Miracle Woman'**
> 'Miracle diet to cure Miracle Woman' became Gurdev's slogan after doctors refused to invest time on healing a 105-year-old cancer patient. It was time for Maan to stick to the basics and focus on high-quality food. Discontinuing her regular athletic diet, a meal plan for cancer patients was prescribed for her. Handling this radical shift especially during the lockdown, took a toll on his health too!

The sack of wheat stored in his living room was no longer required, and he substituted it with *bajra* and *kodra* flour. He eliminated sugar and dairy products completely from her diet. Kefir was no longer her early morning drink. Instead, he served her pomegranate juice mixed with protein powder. Carrot and broccoli-leaf juice became her evening drink. This planned diet worked well and there was a sign of recovery. She gained three kilograms in a span of four weeks!

There were festive celebrations for what turned out to be her last birthday on Earth on 1 March, 2021 and the Universe had made it memorable as she was able to celebrate her day surrounded by her loving family. She enjoyed Women's Day, too, but missed addressing her admirers and interacting with the crowds that she had got accustomed to. Her illness had left her with very little energy, still music did not leave her and she sang with her loved ones surrounding her bed. She remembered folk songs of her times and this was taken as a positive indication that there were no signs of memory loss. For the last few months of her treatment, her family had been visiting her regularly, including several others who would come with suggestions of novel treatments. But her lack of activity was a deterrent as also the subsequent Covid waves that followed that confined her to her apartment. Her regular training and walks were interrupted, and with no physical activity, her muscles atrophied. This further added to her agony as she had no strength left to even do household chores.

Gurdev could not stand the hardships his mother was going through. He had never seen her in such a vulnerable condition. After the muscle loss, she started losing weight. He decided he had to seek help. This time, he went to Himachal Pradesh to consult Ayurvedic doctors who were known to use herbal formulations and yoga to cure such diseases. Gurdev was hoping for treatment, but the doctors gave him no hope and could not prescribe anything. He refused to accept defeat. He took to social media and spread the news of Maan's illness to the world.

Shortly, after, he received a positive response from Shuddhi hospital in Dera Bassi, a city near Chandigarh. Doctors approved Maan's admission and Ayurvedic treatment was started. 'You will see your mother running in the Japan Olympics,' said one of the doctors treating Maan.

Gurdev's heart was once again filled with hope. He did not leave his mother's side and stayed in the hospital premises with her. She began responding positively to the treatment, and after two weeks, she began to feel better. But this improvement was temporary, and soon her feeble body was struggling to keep the deadly disease at bay. Even her youthful heart was now finding it difficult to cope with this virulent form of cancer. By this time, she was very weak and had lost all her muscle mass. Gurdev felt that she had very limited time left. One afternoon around 1 pm, on 31 July, she left the world permanently, after her brave heart failed her. Gurdev was with her as she breathed her last breath. Her son had tried his best, but eventually, he had to bow down to fate.

Maan Kaur was a true *Gurmukh,* who was attuned to the Will of the Guru and had engaged herself to live according to the Guru's teachings. Thus, with a controlled mind and no expectations and desires, her whole life was dedicated to the service of mankind. She had attempted to liberate not only herself, but the whole world by setting up a milestone in sports, and through her motivating speeches that were interspersed with words from the holy book of the Sikhs.

She was a sincere believer in *Chardikala;* her mind never admitted defeat and refused to be crushed by adversities. Nothing could frighten her or dampen her spirits. She remained stable and steadfast in the face of all odds and embodied the universal spirit of tolerance even a century earlier in the age of superstition and the *parda* system.

Maan was destined to experience fame and serve society. She was a role model not just for elders, but also for young athletes, women and mothers, and for spiritual seekers. Who would have imagined that a simple woman with no formal education would be inaugurating prestigious events, or win innumerable medals, not just in the sporting arena but even awards such as the Nari Shakti Puraskar. This miracle woman had no demands and no complaints and accepted life as it came, one day at a time. Maan lived up to her name and also died with it! She made the whole country proud! One word to summarise Maan's life, and her final message to the world was—to be in a state of:

CHARDIKALA
Always In High Spirits

EPILOGUE
A SALUTE TO A SPECIAL WOMAN

The four important phases of human life: birth, initiation, marriage and death incorporate specific rites, and practices across cultures. There are rituals and customs followed at birth, marriage and finally, death. Every culture has its own way of mourning and bidding farewell to the deceased.

Subsequent to the rituals, Gurdev stood watching his mother placed on the bier before moving to the cremation ground.

On 1 August, 2021, Maan was cremated at the Chandigarh crematorium in Sector 25. Gurdev performed the last rites, and with a heavy heart, bid his final goodbyes and lit the pyre. Fans eager to meet Maan were restrained from entering into the hospital boundaries, but no one could stop them from reaching the cremation ground. Along with her family and friends, young athletes, coaches, and politicians paid homage to Maan on her final journey. It was the kind of farewell that Maan's soul would have desired. She was born a loner, but received a ceremonial departure, surrounded by her loved ones on all four sides.

All along, Maan's success stories and upcoming events had been shared on social media, but this time, Gurdev was reluctant to share the news about her departure. He had never witnessed his mother slowing down and it was difficult for him to face the reality of her death. It seemed that just a few weeks ago, she had been mentally preparing herself to compete in the Olympics. Although her illness had prepared her loved ones and well-wishers for the final passing, it took Gurdev a while to move on. After a week, I had spoken to him and all he said was: 'My mother might have survived longer if I would have taken her home and fed and nourished her with homecooked meals. Her cardiac arrest was due to a low protein diet at the hospital and much of this was avoidable and curable at home. Maybe her time had come and the ones left behind only have ifs and buts with themselves, and I am one of them.'

Maan's sports journey had catapulted her into stardom and placed her under the overwhelming glare of the media. Plenty of unwanted questions had come up for the mother-son duo. Gurdev had bristled under one such question— 'Are you not afraid of taking your centenarian mother to such grand international events to run? What if something happens to her? She is surviving because she is running. The day she will stop, life might stop.' How true were those words. When she stopped going to the training ground, her age and the cells of her body started to deteriorate with each passing day.

Soon the news had spread around the whole nation. The people of Punjab expressed their condolences as soon as news of her death surfaced on social media. 'World Masters gold medal winner Maan Kaur, 105, passes away'[1] read a tribute in *The Indian Express,* one that was thoroughly deserved. Obituaries also appeared in *Hindu, Outlook, Hindustan Times, The Tribune,* and *The Times of India,* bidding final adieu to the veteran athlete on behalf of the country. Dignitaries from all over the world expressed their sympathies and condolences.

On an easel at the entrance of the Gurudwara Sri Arjan Sahib Dev ji, Maan's big portrait in her iconic blue India jersey welcomed more than five hundred people who had gathered for Maan's Bhog ceremony in Chandigarh. For a while, I stood staring at her photo and on hearing the hymns, a feeling of connection with the divine evoked, bringing my thoughts back to the present. In Sikh tradition, mourning, lamentation or wailing is discouraged after death, hence grief is symbolically expressed through the singing of holy hymns and a hymn from *Asa Ki Var* (a morning congregational composition of 24 *pauris* or stanzas) struck a chord with the congregation:

> *Kūr rājā kūr parajā kūr sabh sansār*
> *Kūr maṇḍap kūr māṛī kūr baisaṇahār*
> *Kūr suinā kūr rupā kūr paiṇaṇahār*
> *Kūr kāiā kūr kapaṛ kūr rūp apār*
> *Kūr mīā kūr bībī khap hōē khār*
> *Kūri kūrai nēh lagā visariā karatār*
> *Kis nāl kīchai dōsatī sabh jag chalaṇahār*
> *Kūr miṭhā kūr mākhiu kūr ḍōbē pūr*
> *Nānak vakhāṇai bēnatī tudh bājh kūrō kūr*[2]
> —**Guru Nanak, Sri Guru Granth Sahib**

In this verse of nine lines, the repetition of the word *kūr* denotes the false possessions and relationships that we claim to own. False is the king, false are the subjects, false is the entire world; false is the mansion, false are the skyscrapers, false are those who live in them; false is the gold, false is the silver, false are those who wear them; false is the body, false are the clothes, false is the boundless beauty of the body; false is the husband, false is the wife, and the one who indulges is distressed; the love of the false is attached to the false and they forget their Creator; with whom shall we form any close or lasting friendships if the entire world is transient? False is the sweetness, false is honey; falsehood drowns entire boatloads of men. Nanak says a prayer that without You, all is false and only false. Thus, the listed temporary possessions are very sweet to us, just like honey. Without realising the presence of the

One (One Universal Force), we drown ourselves in the burden of indulging in these temporary things.

After the kirtan and final prayers, emotional eulogies were delivered by the counsellor of the city and by her close relatives. The gathering spoke not about the pain or grief of losing Maan, but celebrated her incredible journey. A letter of condolence from Captain Amarinder Singh, the former chief minister of Punjab was also read. Whether it is a time of joy or sorrow, the *langar* (community food) is an exemplary practice and plays a prominent role in gurudwaras all over the globe. Her bhog ceremony concluded in a langar hall where a lavish lunch buffet awaited the congregation.

Maan's last words were simple to understand, yet difficult to practice: 'All throughout my life, I have danced and sang like a sausage tree so that neither a thunderstorm nor tough weather could break my spine; I bent as low as the wind forced me and swayed in the direction of the wind, hence, I survived. So, this is what I wish for all of you and my extended dear ones belonging to this planet. One day we all shall die but the end is peaceful when we are successful in giving up all our attachments and this is achieved only when we have given our best shot in every action.' Giving up attachments is a goal that we all might be trying to achieve but that may require not just a lifetime commitment, but one that may take several births to achieve. 'Aiming to achieve this free-flowing lifestyle with one's own efforts might take us ages, but with His benevolence, we can be liberated in a moment from all our sins and attachments,' she would say.

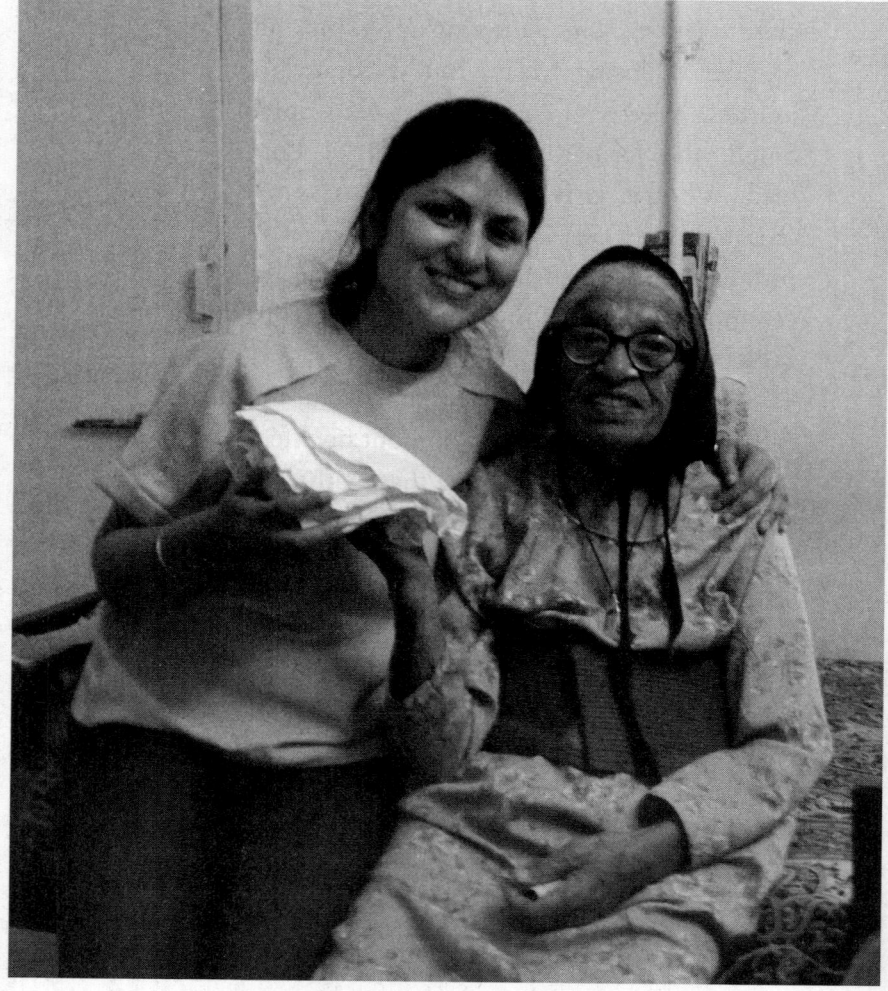

Maan Kaur gifting handcrafted pillow covers to the author

ANNEXURE 1:
RECORDS AND ACHIEVEMENTS

S.No.	Age	Championships	Year	Events
1.	93	National Masters Athletics Championship, Chandigarh	2009	100m-Gold
2.	95	World Masters Athletics Championships, Scramento, USA.	2011	100m-Gold 200m-Gold 400m-Gold
3.	96	Asian Masters Athletics Championships, Taiwan	2012	100m-Gold
4.	97	World Senior Games, Utah, USA	2013	100m-Gold 200m-Gold 400m-Gold Javelin Throw-Gold Shot Put-Gold

S.No.	Age	Championships	Year	Events
5.	97	Canadian Masters Athletics Championships	2013	100m-Gold 200m-Gold 400m-Gold Javelin Throw-Gold Shot Put-Gold
6.	100	Americas Masters Games, Vancouver	2016	100m-Gold 200m-gold 400m-Gold
7.	101	World Masters Games, Auckland	2017	100m-Gold 200m-Gold 400m-Gold Javelin Throw-Gold Shot Put-Gold
8.	102	World Masters Athletics Championship, Malaga, Spain	2018	200m-Gold Javelin Throw-Gold Shot Put-Gold
9.	103	World Masters Athletic Championships Indoor (WMACI)-TORUN, Poland	2019	60m-Gold 200m-Gold Javelin Throw-Gold Shot Put-Gold
10.	103	Asian Masters Athletics Championships, Sarawak, Malaysia	2019	100m-Gold 200m-Gold Javelin Throw-Gold Shot Put-Gold

ANNEXURE 2:
AWARDS

1. Nari Shakti Puraskar, 2020
2. Athlete of the Year, Worlds Masters Athletics Championships, Sacramento, USA, 2011
3. World's Fastest Centenarian, Americas Masters Games, Vancouver
4. Huntsman World Senior Games Broken World Record Award, Javelin Throw, 2013
5. Huntsman World Senior Games Broken Record Award, Shot Put, 2013
6. National Record, Limca Book of Records, 2013
7. Lifetime Achievement Awards, Toronto

ACKNOWLEDGEMENTS

The Lord's grace bestowed on me the greatest privilege to serve society. I thank Him for choosing me and sowing the seed of writing this biography within me as we all work under His Will and command.

Run, Dadi, Run! would not have been possible without the help of Maan Kaur (*Biji*) and her son, Gurdev Singh. She always welcomed me warmly at her residence and open-heartedly shared with me, the people, places and events from her past till the time she lived. She had an excellent memory for names and could recall the minutest details of her early years.

I express my deep sense of gratitude to my aunt, Ipninder Kaur Bedi, for her relentless enthusiasm in reading my manuscript in its initial stages and giving me priceless suggestions for improving the language and the content of the book that you now hold in your hands.

At Vitasta Publishing, I am grateful to Renu Kaul Verma, for trusting and realising the need for sharing the inspiring story of a gifted centenarian with the world; thanks also to my executive editor, Reena Singh, for scrutinising the manuscript, word by word, and to Saumya for bringing the manuscript to life. I would also like to acknowledge Dipti Patel for her support.

For their words of wisdom, I will always be grateful to Dr Gurinder Singh and Sr Harbhajan Singh Chopra. Their spiritual guidance provided clarity to my ever-longing and inquisitive mind.

My deepest debt is due to my husband, Amardeep Singh Sethi for his ineffable support and companionship in all my endeavours; and to my sister, Roma Rakhroy, for nurturing my little mind since childhood and my brother, Jashanjot Singh for his encouragement and positivity. Thanks also to my parents, Gurprit Kaur and Prithipal Singh, Jatinder Kaur and Dharambir Singh for their everlasting prayers and care which made this journey so gracious and fulfilling.

END NOTES

Introduction
1. 101 & running (2017) OMG! Yeh Mera India. Meet India's oldest female athlete [Online] History TV18. https://www.facebook.com/historytv18ind/videos/101-running/1648215331879440/?locale=cs_CZ [Accessed 13 April 2019].
2. Salazar, Ariana Monique, Sahgal Neha (2022) 'In India, head coverings are worn by most women, including roughly six-in-ten Hindus'. *Pew Research Center*, 17 February.

Prologue: Unconditional Love
1. Sarabjeet Kaur, personal interview, March 2020.
2. Guru Gobind Singh, *Tav Prasad Savaiye*. Sri Dasam Granth Sahib, pp.13.

Chapter 1: Lonely Child
1. Ojo, O. B. (2022) 'Socio-economic impacts of 1918–19 influenza epidemic in Punjab, *Journal of Asian and African Studies*', vol. 55, no. 7, pp. 1023-1032.

2. Yasmin Robina (2022) *Muslims under Sikh rule in the nineteenth century: Maharaja Ranjit Singh and religious tolerance.* Bloomsbury Publishing.
3. David Page (1999) *Prelude to partition: The Indian Muslims and the imperial system of control.* Oxford India Paperbacks.
4. Bourne, Judith (2023) 'Great expectations and hard times: the advent of the Sex Disqualification (Removal) Act 1919 and women's entry to the legal profession,' *Women's History Review*, vol. 32, no. 6, pp. 793-808.
5. Andiappan P. (1979) 'Public Policy and Sex Discrimination in Employment in India,' *Indian Journal of Industrial Relations*, vol. 14, no. 3, pp. 395 - 415.
6. Ministry of Culture. The life of Sant Kabir Das. Government of India. [Online] Retrieved from https://indianculture.gov.in/stories/life-sant-kabir-das.

Chapter 2: Family

1. Traboulay, David M. (1997) *Mahatma Gandhi's Satyagraha and Nonviolent Resistance.* City University of New York, College of Staten Island.
2. Susan Bean (1989) 'Gandhi and Khadi: The Fabric of Indian Independence,' in Annette B. Weiner and Jane Schneider eds., *Cloth and Human Experience.* Washington D.C.: Smithsonian Institution Press, pp. 368.
3. M.K. Gandhi (1968) *The voice of truth.* Navajivan Publishing House, pp. 309.

4. Rothermund D. (1980) 'The Impact of the Great Depression on India in the 1930s,' in Proceedings of the Indian History Congress, vol. 41, pp. 657- 669.

Chapter 3: Maharaja Bhupinder Singh

1. Gurpreetinder Sekhon (2023) 'Development of the artistic and cultural traditions in Patiala state (1820-1947): The contribution of Patiala rulers towards development of art and cultural traditions in Patiala,' *International Journal of Creative Research Thoughts*, vol. 11, no. 7.
2. Natwar K. Singh (1998) *The Magnificent Maharaja*. Harper Collins Publishers.
3. Amrtansh Arora (2023) 'Maharaja Bhupinder Singh, patron saint of Patiala peg who used Sikh identity to his advantage.' *The Print*, 23 March.
4. Khushwant Singh (2022) 'Exhausted Highness: A sanitised biography of a colourful, yet despicable ruler.' *Outlook*, 6 February.
5. Dass J. Diwan (1981) *Maharaja*. Allied Publishers Private Limited.
6. Khushwant Singh (2022) 'Exhausted Highness: A sanitised biography of a colourful, yet despicable ruler.' *Outlook*, 6 February.
7. Sartaj Chaudhary (2016) 'Once upon a time there was a King.' *The Tribune*, 3 June.
8. Ibid.

9. Cartier F. B. (2021) *The Cartiers: The untold story of the family behind the jewelry empire*. Ballantine Books.
10. Amin Jaffer, Pramod K. G., Martand Singh and Shilpa Vijayakrishnan (2015) 'Portrait of Rani Yashoda Devi of Patiala.' Vandyk Studios, London. In Maharanis: Women of Royal India, Museum of Art & Photography.
11. The News Himachal (2021) 'Chail Palace gets heritage status.' *The News Himachal*, 16 March.
12. Lara Rebello (2012) 'Quick getaway: Mulshi dam, Chail.' *The Economic Times*, 12 April.
13. Gurpreetinder Sekhon (2023) 'Development of the artistic and cultural traditions in Patiala state (1820-1947). The contribution of Patiala rulers towards development of art and cultural traditions in Patiala,' *International Journal of Creative Research Thoughts*, vol. 11, no. 7.
14. Amrtansh Arora (2023) 'Maharaja Bhupinder Singh, patron saint of Patiala peg who used Sikh identity to his advantage.' *The Print*, 23 March.

Chapter 4: Divided India and Love

1. Phillips Sean (2017) *Why was British India partitioned in 1947? Considering the role of Muhammad Ali Jinnah*. Faculty of History, University of Oxford.
2. Ibid.
3. Sangeet Toor (2021) 'A century apart, currents of dissent bridge the farmers' protests and the Muzara Movement.' *The Caravan*, 25 February.

4. Paramjit Singh (2022) 'Punjab's Peasant Movements Past and Present,' *Economic and Political Weekly*, vol. 67, no. 23, pp. 27-29.
5. Sangeet Toor (2021) 'A century apart, currents of dissent bridge the farmers' protests and the Muzara Movement.' *The Caravan*, 25 February.
6. Vishav Bharti (2017) 'Punjabi journalism 150 years old, but nobody remembers', *The Tribune*, 11 December.
7. Ibid.
8. Ibid.
9. Harminder Singh (2014) 'Development of Punjabi journalism during freedom struggle in Punjab,' *International Research Journal of Management Sociology & Humanity*, vol. 5, no. 12, pp. 172-184.
10. Busharat E Jamil (2015) 'Religious minorities in Pakistan Sikh Enigma: The dissection of Punjab 1947,' *Journal of the Punjab University Historical Society*, vol. 28, no.1.
11. Datta, V. N. (1998) 'The Punjab Boundary Commission Award (12 August, 1947), in Proceedings of the Indian History Congress,' vol. 59, pp. 850 - 62.
12. Ilyas Chattha (2021) 'Some fruits of freedom: Partition and the history of evacuee property in Pakistan,' *Journal of Migration Affairs*, vol. 4, no. 1, pp. 36-53.
13. William Dalrymple (2015) 'The great divide: The violent legacy of Indian Partition.' *The New Yorker*, 29 June.

14. Ilyas Chattha(2021) 'Some fruits of freedom: Partition and the history of evacuee property in Pakistan,' *Journal of Migration Affairs*, vol. 4, no. 1, pp. 36-53.
15. Gyanendra Pandey (2001) *Remembering Partition: Violence, nationalism, and history in India*. Cambridge University Press.
16. Department of Food, Civil Supplies and Consumer Affairs. (2019-2020) *Annual Report*. Government of Punjab.
17. Hengul J. Das (2017) 'Chail Gurudwara Saheb.' *The Times of India*, 21 June.
18. Lamont Thomas (2014) 'Give me blood, and I will give you freedom: Bhagat Singh, Subhas Chandra Bose, and the uses of violence in India's Independence movement,' *Education About ASIA*, vol. 19, no. 1, pp. 5-10.
19. Iftikhar, Anam, Chawla, Iqbal Muhammad (2018) 'Re-contextualizing Bhagat Singh's freedom struggle for independence of India,' *Journal of the Research Society of Pakistan*, vol. 55, no. 1, pp. 17-30.
20. Namita Vijay Dharia (2022) *The Industrial Ephemeral: Labor and love in Indian architecture and construction*. Berkeley: University of California Press, pp. 201-206
21. Randhir Singh (1993) *Autobiography of Bhai Sahib Randhir Singh*. Ludhiana: Bhai Sahib Randhir Singh Trust.
22. Ibid.
23. Bhagat Singh (1931) 'Why I am an Atheist,' *The People*, 27 September, pp. 195-201.

Chapter 5: Gurdev with a Twist

1. Monisha Kumar and Amita Wali (2016) 'Elucidation of the Indian salwar kameez,' *International E-Journal of Advances in Social Sciences*, vol. 2, no. 6, pp. 753-761.

Chapter 6: God Proposes, Wo-Maan Runs!

1. Guru Nanak, *Jap Ji Sahib*, Sri Guru Granth Sahib, pp. 3.

Chapter 8: Hollow Bones and a Fresh Start

1. Ravneet Singh (2023). 'Punjabi University gets 'A+' NAAC accreditation.' *The Tribune*, 12 October.

Chapter 9: A Novel Experiment

1. Li R., Dai Y., Han Y., Zhang C., Pang J., Li J., Zhang T. and Zeng P. (2023) 'Doing housework and having regular daily routine stand out as factors associated with physical function in older people'. *Front. Public Health*, 28 November.
2. Ausland A., Sandberg E. L., Jortveit J. and Seiler S. (2022) 'Heart rhythm assessment in elite endurance athletes: A better method?' *Front. Sports Act, Living*, 25 July.

Chapter 10: The First Run

1. Harvard Medical School (2014) 'Exercise and Aging: Can you walk away from father time.' *Harvard Health Publishing*, 9 March.

Chapter 11: Out of Patiala
1. Guru Nanak, *Jap Ji Sahib*. Sri Guru Granth Sahib, pp. 8.

Chapter 13: *Digdi Haan, te Jitdi Haan*—I fall, so I win!
1. Harbans Lal (2013) 'Waheguru: The ineffable Divine Light'. *SikhNet*, 29 October.
2. Guru Arjan Dev, *Sri Guru Granth Sahib*, pp. 618.

Chapter 14: Hole in a Pocket
1. Keshav Singh (2021) 'Vice and virtue in Sikh ethics', *The Monist*, vol. 104, No. 3, pp. 319 - 336.
2. Guru Nanak, *Jap Ji Sahib*, Sri Guru Granth Sahib, pp. 2.

Chapter 15: What made Maan Run?
1. Arvind-Pal Singh Mandair (2017). Shabad (Word), Sikhism. In: Mandair, A.P.S. (eds) Sikhism. Encyclopedia of Indian Religions. Springer, Dordrecht. https://doi.org/10.1007/978-94-024-0846-1_486.

Chapter 16: Maan's Secrets to Longevity
1. Dharmender Kumar and Mukherjee Doel (2024), 'The Causes and trends in the arrivals of apple and tomato to some selected sub-market yards of Himachal Pradesh,' *Current Agriculture Research Journal*, vol. 12, no. 1, pp. 474-484.
2. Giovanni Schepici, Placido Bramanti, and Emanuela Mazzon (2020) 'Efficacy of sulforaphane in

neurodegenerative diseases', *International Journal of Molecular Sciences*, vol. 21, no. 22, pp. 8637.
3. Rosa, D. D. et al. (2017) 'Milk kefir: nutritional, microbiological and health benefits', *Nutrition Research Reviews*, vol. 30, no. 1, pp. 82-96.
4. Je-Ruei Liu, Sheng-Yao Wang, Yuh-Yih Lin, Chin-Wen Lin (2002) 'Antitumor activity of milk kefir and soy milk kefir in tumor-bearing mice', *Nutrition and Cancer*, vol. 44, no. 2, pp. 183-187.
5. Shubhajit Sarkhel, Dronachari Manvi, Ramachandra C. T. (2020) 'Nutrition importance and health benefits of mulberry leaf extract: A review', *Journal of Pharmacognosy and Phytochemistry*, vol. 9, no. 5, pp. 689-695.
6. Diksha Manaware (2020) 'Drumstick (Moringa oleifera): A miracle tree for its nutritional and pharmaceutic properties', *International Journal of Current Microbiology and Applied Sciences*, vol. 9, no. 9, pp. 41-50.
7. Renu Mogra and Preeti Rathi (2013) 'Health benefits of wheat grass—a wonder food', *International Journal of Food and Nutritional Sciences*, vol.2, no. 4, pp. 10-13.

Chapter 17: Maan, a Valued Celebrity!
1. Sikh Reht Maryada, Amrit Sanskar: Ceremony of Khande di Pahul. https://old.sgpc.net/sikhism/amrit-sanskar.asp.
2. Vaisakhi: origins of the Khalsa (2009), BBC. https://www.bbc.co.uk/religion/religions/sikhism/holydays/vaisakhi.shtml.

3. Nari Shakti Puraskar. Ministry of Women and Child Development. New Delhi: Government of India.

Chapter 18: Room Number One

1. Mona Sood and Harveen Bhandari (2023), 'Exploring the significance of historic gardens in context to cultural diversity: The case of the royal gardens of Punjab,' *ShodhKosh: Journal of Visual and Performing Arts*, vol. 4, no. 2, pp. 95-106.
2. Patiala, *The Sikh Encyclopaedia;* https://www.thesikhencyclopedia.com/other-historical-places/punjab/patiala/.

Chapter 21: The Last Run

1. Burak Mete, Ferdi Tanir, and Hakan Demirhindi (2022) 'Impact of the COVID-19 pandemic on frailty in older adults', *European Journal of Geriatrics and Gerontology*, vol. 4, no. 2, pp. 79-84.

Epilogue: A Salute to a Special Woman

1. Nitin Sharma (2021) 'World Masters gold medal winner Maan Kaur, 105, passes away'. *The Indian Express*, 31 July.
2. Guru Nanak, *Asa Ki Vaar*. Sri Guru Granth Sahib, pp. 468.

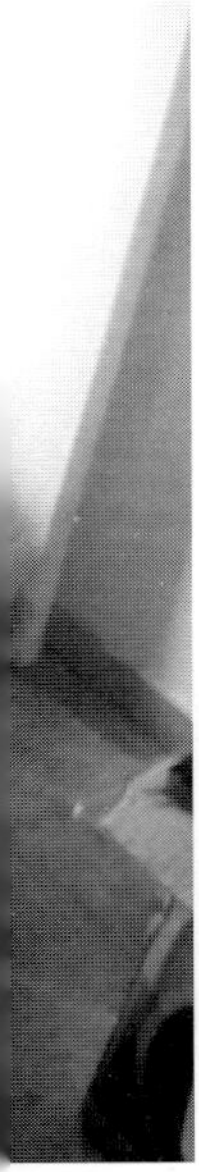

Captions Below

1. Maan Kaur with her son
2. Walking the ramp with Milind Soman
3. Maan's laboratory
4. Jo Bole So Nihal Sat Sri Akal at WMA
5. Wheat batter
6. At the Auckland Sky Tower
7. Wheat grass for juice
8. Kefir, Maan's superfood
9. With her love—sewing machine
10. Wheat batter chapati with sarson da saag
11. Relishing her midday meal—Horse gram
12. Maan's research room
13. Herbs, dried leaves and flowers in her refrigerator